Prosperity Unbound

With the support of INSEAD Euro-Asia and Comparative Research Centre and special thanks to Gordon Redding and Charlotte Butler.

Prosperity Unbound

Building Property Markets With Trust

Elena Panaritis

First published 2007 by
PALGRAVE MACMILLAN
Houndmills, Basingstoke, Hampshire RG21 6XS and
175 Fifth Avenue, New York, N. Y. 10010
Companies and representatives throughout the world

PALGRAVE MACMILLAN is the global academic imprint of the Palgrave
Macmillan division of St. Martin's Press, LLC and of Palgrave Macmillan Ltd.
Macmillan® is a registered trademark in the United States, United Kingdom
and other countries. Palgrave is a registered trademark in the European
Union and other countries.

ISBN-13: 978–1–4039–9346–5   hardback
ISBN-10: 1–4039–9346–7   hardback

This book is printed on paper suitable for recycling and made from fully
managed and sustained forest sources.

A catalogue record for this book is available from the British Library.

Library of Congress Cataloging-in-Publication Data
    Panaritis, Elena, 1968–
    Prosperity unbound : building property markets with trust / Elena
    Panaritis.
        p. cm.
    Includes bibliographical references and index.
    ISBN-13: 978–1–4039–9346–5   (cloth)
    ISBN-10: 1–4039–9346–7   (cloth)
        1. Informal sector (Economics) 2. Right of property. 3. Economic
    development. I. Title

    HD2341.P355 2007
    330–dc22   2006050306

10   9   8   7   6   5   4   3   2   1
16   15   14   13   12   11   10   09   08   07

Printed and bound in Great Britain by
Antony Rowe Ltd, Chippenham and Eastbourne

To my parents Elli and Yiannis

Contents

List of Figures

Foreword

It has now been well over a decade since the development policy community begun to concentrate on the questions of institutions and governance as one of the keys to economic growth. During the late 1980s and early 1990s, much of the focus was on shifting policies in an economically orthodox direction, meaning policy emphasis on a reduction of the size of the state sector, liberalization of prices, and reduction of various tariffs, licences, and fees by which governments generated rents and favored particular market participants. While orthodox structural adjustment in a number of Latin American countries following the debt crisis of the early 1980s succeeded in stabilizing their macroeconomies, there was a realization that stability and openness by itself was often not sufficient to bring about rapid economic growth. Many countries did not have the proper institutional environment under which policy change would make a difference. Indeed, in a number of countries, premature liberalization of capital accounts or privatization of state assets, created new problems when government authorities did not have the capacity to regulate banks or stage transparent auctions.

There has been a substantial body of academic research accumulated on the relationship between institutions and economic growth, which originated in the theoretical perspective provided by Douglass North's new institutional economics. North pointed out the limitations of the traditional neoclassical model that assumed perfect information and zero transaction costs, conditions that seldom appeared in developed economies and were never present in less developed ones. Work by economists like Daron Acemoglu, James Robinson, William Easterly, and Ross Levine has tended to underline the importance of property rights and a rule of law that could uphold them. The new realization that "institutions mattered" reached a broader audience in the writings of Hernando de Soto, whose book *The Other Path* pointed to weak legal regimes as a source of informality, and whose 1998 work *The Mystery of Capital* pointed to the importance of property rights for the poor.

The World Bank's 1997 World Development Report, entitled *The State in a Changing World*, was an important milestone in the shift to concern for institutions. While continuing to emphasize openness as a source of growth, this report noted that states remained critical as providers of public goods, and for their ability to resolve social conflicts. The Bank began to emphasize public sector reform in its lending, providing technical assistance to projects that sought to help countries fight corruption, strengthen judicial systems, and build capacity in basic financial management. It has also funded projects seeking to reform property rights, including the project in Peru that is described in detail in this book.

While the intellectual justification for an emphasis on property rights is clear, institutional reform as a practical matter has been much more difficult to carry out. There are a number of reasons for this. One is the fact that the optimal design of institutions is often unclear. Many institutional reformers have as models the kinds of political, legal, or administrative systems that exist in developed Western societies, which they seek to transport to societies with very different social and cultural backgrounds. An institution that works in Europe or North America often has surprising effects when applied in contexts lacking their dense, interconnected institutional ecology. Institutions therefore have to be modified to take account of local conditions, but that kind of knowledge is often lacking on the part of well-meaning outsiders.

A second reason why donor-driven institutional reform fails has to do with the problem of ownership. The demand for institutions must come from within the society if they are to be sustainable, but such demand is often not forthcoming. Institutions imposed as conditions for lending are often skirted, distorted, or else simply ignored. The same holds true for institutions imposed during occupations, or in the course of post-conflict interventions on the part of the international community.

A third problem has to do with the interconnected nature of institutions. Property rights, for example, arise out of the interplay of a number of different institutions. There must be a formal titling authority, for example, and a government capacity to maintain property records which some countries are notorious for losing or deliberately destroying. But titles need to be connected to a functioning judicial system if they are to have meaning, a judicial system that can adjudicate disputes in a timely and fair manner, free from interference by interested political authorities.

A final problem has to do with politics. Weak or missing institutions are often the result not of ignorance or incapacity; they are the outcomes of choices deliberately made by political actors. Corruption in a public bureaucracy, for example, is often the result of a political leader seeking to pack the government with kinsmen or co-ethnics in order to enhance the leader's power. Incumbent office holders seldom have strong incentives to change the rules by which they came to power. But outside development agencies and donors often do not have either the power or the mandate to intervene in local politics in ways that will get to the root of these institutional dysfunctions.

It is in the context of the practical problem of building institutions that *Prosperity Unbound* is particularly
welcome. Elena Panaritis has had long on-the-ground
experience in property rights / institutional reform
work; her work in Peru forms one of the case studies
around which this book is built. Her "reality check"
approach is an effort to give practitioners a straight-
forward set of guidelines on how to enter into an institutional reform. It takes account of the need for partners,
and for getting the politics of reform right, as well as
the need to tailor the project to local conditions. Her
approach moreover recognizes the fact that not all such
intentions are feasible, and thus provides parameters
for understanding where and when they should be
attempted.

Prosperity Unbound is a very significant contribution
to a growing literature on institutional reform as a key
component of economic development. While remain-
ing well grounded in theory, it goes well beyond the
existing theoretical literature to provide practical advice
for how reform can be carried out. As without the ability
to translate these ideas into practice, the potential of contemporary market-driven growth will never be realized.

Francis Fukuyama

Prologue

Knowing that you own the house you live in and the land that your family has occupied for many years means that you can relocate to live or work in another city or country, secure in the knowledge that your property will still belong to you when you return. It also means you can sell your land or use it as collateral to acquire other assets, for example, to start a business. These assurances have a profound effect on individual mobility and economic behavior.

Residents of informal settlements live in a world of uncertainty and limited choices. They may not be able to leave their homes unattended for even a day without fear of it being taken over by other homeless settlers. Options for improving their lives are few: Should I invest in improving my house by building another room or by installing running water and electricity? Will my vote count in local elections? Will my needs and preferences for services like schools for my children and waste collection be represented in local government plans? A citizen's legitimate claim to title is at the center of these fundamental questions of voice and self determination. Neither residents nor local entrepreneurs will invest in communities that are insecure.

Increased migration to urban areas has led to growing numbers of informal settlements around the world. According to UN Habitat, in 2003 there were 924 million people living in slums, nearly 95 percent of whom were in developing and transition economies. Slum dwellers lack basic services and suffer enormous hardship as a result. Only 32 percent have access to safe water, while the world average for urban residents is 76 percent.

Similarly, only 20 percent of this group have access to sewerage, compared to 64 percent on average for urban residents worldwide. In sub-Saharan Africa, 70 percent of urban residents live in slums. In Nairobi, for example, if you live in a slum, your children are almost three times as likely to die before they are five as are the children of formal city residents.

Prosperity Unbound presents a fresh perspective on the issues of informality and property. The book's main contribution is its assessment of the legal, regulatory, and institutional reforms and policies that are needed to convert informal real estate or the "unreal estate" as the author terms it, into formal real estate. In addition to examples of successful approaches to reform, the author provides a diagnostic tool that is not only well-grounded in theory but also designed for use by practitioners.

This book will be of interest to a broad and diverse readership: policymakers in developed countries looking for solutions for depressed urban neighborhoods; policymakers in developing countries seeking to improve the business environment and provide better access to assets for the poor; and concerned citizens who are looking for ways to secure their savings and investments, to increase their mobility, or to have their voices heard. Real estate investors exploring new markets and ways of combining social value with profit making will also find the book stimulating, as will economist and students interested in institutional reform, societal transformation, and informality in real property markets.

Frannie Léautier
Vice President of the World Bank Institute

Introduction: Why have I written this book?

This book is about property, informality, and institutions. In a world of informality, people live and work outside the formal market structures. It is not a well understood concept and even less well addressed. Informality of property and property rights, affects markets and society.

A solution to this "problem" does exist however, and transformation is possible, all the while offering opportunities for financial, economic and social returns. The book charts the transformation of informal property – which I call "unreal estate" – to formal property, or real estate, through a deep, institutional change in property rights.

Why should informal property be transformed? Some estimate that more than 50 percent of the world's population lives and works on informal properties. Informally-held property results in undervalued and distressed real estate. The prevalence of unreal estate is a bottleneck to growth and prosperity worldwide, making it a social issue as well as a significant economic and financial problem. Informal property is a phenomenon that recognizes no geographic boundaries. It is found in developing countries, yet it is also present, in different ways but for the same reasons, in urban and rural areas in the developed world.

Why should we transform informality now? While the problem of informality in real estate is not new, it is increasingly relevant as globalization and its associated greater information flows have fallen short of expectations that they would expand markets and create more wealth. Awareness of the problem has risen, but a solution has remained elusive, contributing only to increased frustration and disappointment.

We are facing long-standing expectations for a solution and growing impatience. Reform in the area of institutions, especially property rights is essential to this effort. However, it has not yet happened. In fact, conventional efforts to address unreal estate through government housing policies and programs, or through titling programs, do not make private sector involvement competitive, ultimately dampening property ownership and transfer. Such technical responses tend to fail to address the fundamental causes of informal property ownership in a long-term, sustainable way. Clearly, a different approach is needed.

Some argue that the problem of informality is essentially unsolvable, believing the root cause is a cultural one. I have a different view. I suggest that informality arises from the mismatch of institutions, organizations and society's demands, and the repairing of malfunctioning institutions requires profound reforms. How does this mismatch come about? How can the appropriate reform take place?

I seek to answer these questions using a new analytical tool, Reality Check Analysis, which diagnoses unhealthy institutions that spawn and perpetuate informality, the first step in transforming unreal estate into formal property. This tool, introduced in this book, was born of both practice and theory. The work on these pages complements writings on the importance of institutions in markets, books that have raised awareness of the issue of informality and property along with hopes for a solution, and writings that have introduced the concept of institutions as a key element of successful market reform.

Transforming unreal estate to real estate brings changes, large and small, touching individual lives and entire societies. It offers people who own and use property a *real choice* over their property assets and increases trust in the security of their savings and wealth. It gives property owners more freedom regarding where they work and a greater voice in their own society. This very transformation occurred in Peru, which undertook a nationwide reform of its property rights system in the 1990s.

Peru's reforms, written into its constitution and legal structure, meant so much more than mere changes in law. Peru was transformed at a deep institutional level. The way Peruvians conducted formal transactions related to their homes, their land, their communities and their savings started to change unalterably. Naturally, there was resistance. At times, I wondered if I would ever see the changes happen. Opposition and criticism from some corners of the Peruvian Government, policymakers, and even the Peruvian terrorists was fervent and undeniable. On several occasions, I was wondering if I would ever see the changes happen. Yet the push for reform would have not been possible on willpower alone. In the end it was the forged partnerships and the team created around the project of reform that pushed the effort forward. For all their opposition, the naysayers could not drown out the momentum that stemmed from the immediate beneficiaries, namely property owners and private sector investors. Reality Check Analysis worked in Peru, proving that even in an environment where the conventional wisdom suggests that little can be done, a great transformation can be wrought.

This experience showed that policymakers, governments, private investors and entrepreneurs can begin tapping resources in a way that benefits individuals, groups and whole societies. This outcome is also evident in the transformation of distressed neighborhoods of the US and Europe, examples of which I present in this book. Through such examples, the book shows how to move beyond conventional strategies to bring about an institutional *shakeup*, and invites groups to come together with the common purpose of increasing access to formal markets and creating a stronger economy.

The transformation of informal property into formal property is possible if the essential ingredients, outlined in these pages, are present. This book is addressed to the concerned citizen, investor, economist, policymaker, government official and anyone interested in the implications of informality in markets and real estate. I ask you to leave your preconceptions behind as we travel on this journey and observe the effects of unreal estate on the rich and poor, investors, citizens and the State. Although some of the sights will be gloomy, the road ahead is an exciting one, offering opportunities for those in the public and private sectors willing to take this path.

Investors may find this book revealing for its fresh view on property and property rights reform, highlighting the potential for financial and social returns by investing in previously informal properties in a nontraditional way. It is especially directed to those with the vision to add value by creating value. Moreover, investors' interest in expanding property markets can spur policymakers to commit to the deep institutional reforms needed to achieve the transformation of unreal estate to real estate.

Policymakers will be introduced to a different "how" in institutional reforms, one based on institutions as a representation of social needs. Institutions have begun to appear on policymakers' radar screens, a good development, but one that does not go far enough. We need to do more, or we will keep on asking the wrong questions and offering the wrong solutions. I cannot claim that misaligned institutions and property rights are the causes of all the world's miseries, but certainly they are the cause of many, including reduced productivity, opportunistic behavior, mismanagement and corruption.

Today, Peru's reform process is ongoing and its successes continue long after the initial impetus had evaporated. The transformation that occurred there can happen elsewhere, and this book is a call to all those who wish to undertake similar efforts. The first chapters present the conceptual and practical boundaries of informality, while later chapters focus on how to bring about such a transformation, presenting examples from Peru, the US and Europe. The book concludes with a discussion of underlying principles and strategy, highlighting what the experience of institutional reforms means for the rest of the world. Taking this journey I hope you will come away with practical solutions to reforming institutions, including property rights, and open the door to unbound prosperity.

1
Informality and Unreality

> *Any person ought to have the right to enjoy the fruits of his own work.*
>
> – David Hume

Informal markets permeate economies worldwide. Informality coexists with formal market structures in developing and developed countries alike, making assets illiquid and locking up potential profits. What does informality look like? It has a very human face. Picture Latin America, where farmers sell produce on a side street without a license. Picture Europe where new, often undocumented immigrants hawk items at outdoor bazaars or at street intersections in large cities whenever traffic is stopped. Picture New York City, where drivers without a hackney license use their own cars as taxis after finishing their "regular" job. Picture "transaction middle men," ubiquitous in Latin America, where they usually are referred to by the elegant Spanish name of *tramitadores,* who are hired by wealthier citizens for help with seemingly simple tasks such as renewing a passport or obtaining a government license. Picture New Orleans, where some residents reportedly refused to leave their homes after hurricane Katrina hit in the fall of 2005 because they did not have official documentation proving their ownership. Many transactions to transfer, buy or sell properties in the city were not registered but kept in personal notarized contracts, which were in danger of being lost in the floodwaters.

Informality is social and economic behavior or conduct under rules recognized only among the members of a community – and it has consequences. In informal markets, people have marketable assets that are not properly licensed or registered, and they also buy, sell, own or lease real estate without registering the transaction. In a market setting, informality prevents individuals from enforcing or defending their rights and excludes their labor and assets from formal transactions. The result is that the value for their work and property is set at a lower level than what their "true" value would be in a formal market.

The concept of informality can be difficult to understand, particularly for those who live and work in the developed world, and even for some of those who live and work within the formal structures of developing economies that also have parallel informal markets. It can seem naive, foreign, irrational and marginal. It can even appear folkloric.

For many, participation in informal markets is not a choice, but a reflection of the absence of choice. It is a pragmatic survival mechanism for those excluded from formal markets by a lack of information and prohibitively high costs, two factors which also can quickly squeeze individuals out of formal markets they struggled to enter. Exclusion is a key element of informality. This soon leads to a situation in which formal and informal markets exist in parallel, but with stunted profits in both, and forces the creation of alternative enforcement mechanisms for informal systems and transactions, because participants in these markets cannot rely on formal avenues of redress.

In the aggregate, informality wastes resources and imposes far greater costs than providing equal access for all to formal markets. These costs are borne by the individual and society as a whole. The cost of informal markets is found in the difficulty of enforcing rights over labor and assets, which makes employment precarious, raises transactions costs and lowers asset values.[1] Formal institutions have a better track record of reducing transactions costs than do informal institutions, which explains in part why assets tend to be more valuable in formal than in informal markets.

As pervasive as it is, informality is difficult to quantify. Consider, though, one attempt to gauge its impact on property. According to an estimate by de Soto, the worldwide cost of construction materials locked in buildings that are considered "informal" and hence illiquid, is $9.3 trillion, which de Soto explains is "nearly as much as the total value of all the companies listed on the main stock exchanges of the world's twenty most developed countries."[2]

Informality and Illegality

Often, informality in markets is equated with illegality, which is not always the case. While informality takes place beyond the confines of the law, the "informal way" is not necessarily against or in violation of the law. To be informal does not necessarily mean one is illegal, or vice versa.

There are clear distinctions. Informal markets arise when formal rules are overly restrictive, unclear, unpredictable or costly to follow. Illegality, however, most times includes an element of intent. If one were to cheat the system and register the wrong property in one's name, or fake a title of ownership, that would be illegal.

Informality is very prominent in property and labor markets. When Rita, a seamstress supporting her family, decided to register her small home, she later discovered, to her surprise, that she had embarked on a multi-year marathon. Although Rita has lived in the house for years and dutifully paid

> ## Informality and Illegality – *continued*
>
> her property taxes, she found that the institutional structure made it almost impossible to move into the formal world. Rules that were confusing to begin with changed and she was forced to start over. Then, she was told that she had been violating the rules and faced a fine. Without the luxury of time and money to hire lawyers, go to court and hope to resolve the matter, Rita had no choice but to remain in the informal environment. Instead, like many of her neighbors, she decided to continue to rely on property tax receipts as her "official" proof of ownership.
>
> When José, a day worker of limited means wanted to start a taxi service, he spent months collecting the requisite papers to obtain a taxi license. After repeatedly going back and forth to the license office, an official refused to accept his application. The problem? A discrepancy in the names on his documents. The accent mark was omitted from his name on his identity card, making it slightly different from the name on his driver's license. José was faced with having to petition the civil registry to correct the mistake on his identity card, a time-consuming process that would probably defer his dream by at least a year. His two other options: Bribe the official to overlook the discrepancy and accelerate the process of getting licensed, or forgo the license and instead get a large sheet of paper, write "TAXI" in bold, black letters, and stick it on the front window of his car. We leave you to guess which he chose.

Why are informal markets more prevalent in some countries than in others?

All too commonly, people consider informality to be some sort of cultural phenomenon. We hear informal market behavior characterized, for instance, as the "black market." Those in the formal world often view those who engage in informal markets as having a negative mindset. They may take a facile view of this informal part of the world as a place where people live with values that breed informality. People may see the gap between formal and informal markets as signs of a gap based on race or geography, black versus white, or North versus South. Informality may be described as a "Latin" phenomenon, or an "African" phenomenon, or

---

Asymmetric Information and Moral Hazard Behavior

Information known to some is often unknown to others. The seller of a used car generally has more information about the vehicle than the buyer; for example he may have been the driver in an accident that required rebuilding the entire rear end of the car. The buyer, though, only knows what he is told or is able to find out by inspecting the vehicle before the purchase.[3] This asymmetry of information distorts market participation and market prices as the seller can price the car above the level the buyer would be willing to pay had he had complete information. Obviously, buyers of used cars are not the only ones suffering from incomplete, one-sided information. In fact, asymmetric information can be a serious issue when it is widespread and affects markets across the board and eventually decision-making.

Information asymmetry is frequently accompanied by another problem which economists refer to as moral hazard behavior. Broadly speaking, moral hazard describes a situation in which a party to a contractual relationship, a single person or a group of persons, behaves opportunistically and can affect the outcome of this relationship to its own advantage.[4] Moral hazard behavior usually develops when individuals know that the benefit they expect outweighs any possible negative consequences. For instance, people who have more information than others may have less incentive to share their insights if they wish to use this knowledge for their own private gain.

With regard to informality, asymmetry of information keeps some people who do not have access to all the information necessary to participate in the formal market from enjoying the full benefit of their marketable assets. At the same time, a small privileged elite who does have access to crucial resources has the incentive (moral hazard) to block information flow or even misinform others in order to preserve the status quo which is beneficial to them.

---

just "the way *they* do things." From this perspective, it is a very small leap to conclude that even corruption – a byproduct of informality, one might argue – is part of the social fabric and built into the "social DNA" of these societies and their people.

High transactions costs are evidence of informality and act as barriers to entry. The process of completing one transaction may entail many bureaucratic requirements and continuous demands from officials at any stage of the process for clearances, inspections, documents or witnesses. Sometimes the demands are legitimate and expected; some other times they are unexpected and created on the spot by some official. People – such as Rita or José – often cannot see the end point of a transaction they engage in and determine whether it is worth pursuing without first incurring its exorbitant costs. Transactions costs lead to a limited number of formal players and asymmetry of information. As a result, policy and market decisions tend to be based on information provided by these few formal players and only apply to them, which further distorts values and prices. A vicious circle develops; high transactions costs protect the beneficiaries of the system who can influence policies so as to maintain transaction costs – and thus barriers to entry – high.

If this sounds complicated, it is! The implications of informality have investors view informal markets as risky and unpredictable, making participation in them unattractive. Consequently, private investment into such markets, if any, is confined to small lines of credit or microfinance, usually backed by government guarantees.

As we will see in Chapter 2, informality often springs from abrupt shocks in a country's historical development, such as wars, colonization or occupation, and is hatched by rigid institutions that can be found, for example, in countries with a strong mercantilist tradition.[5] Informality tends to thrive in these types of economies, typically closed to outside influences, or in seemingly open economies where it is well-hidden in the wrinkles of regulated market segments. Thus, informality is not a phenomenon created overnight, but one with deep historical roots. Ultimately, countries with excessive regulation keep their markets working by limiting participation in the formal economy to a small elite. Just as in the centuries-old mercantile world, where Kings, nobles, merchants and priests constituted their own elite, such economies operate as a "members only" club, deriving legitimacy from a privileged group that has both monopoly power and, obviously, an interest in preserving the *status quo*.[6] These economies, although very inefficient, do survive as long as they limit market transactions and keep themselves highly regulated and as closed as possible.

The role of history

When I traveled to Peru in the early 1990s, I was surprised to find remnants of mercantilism still powerful in pockets of the economy and among the elites who sought to guide policy making and control most natural resources and economic activity, including land transactions. Mercantilism was the economic philosophy of the sixteenth, seventeenth and eighteenth centuries in Europe, where the state was expected to be strong and the key players had clearly defined roles in the economy. Kings controlled money and security, nobles controlled agriculture, merchants controlled trade, priests controlled morality and behavior and the serfs served as the labor force.[7] Trade, land and mining were highly regulated and transactions were valued and paid in precious metals. Mercantilists identified these assets with wealth and viewed the economy as a zero sum game in which a gain by one party was a loss by another.

Studying Peru's history and especially the sequence of the country's ruling patterns helped me understand what I had experienced during my visits. The Spanish in America brought a strong mercantilist culture to their colonies in the New World. After exploiting the mines of Mexico and Peru, Spanish colonizers turned to the land and aimed to recreate the great estates of the Castilian nobility in Spain. Spanish colonial societies were based on institutions that mirrored those in Spain. The Council of the Indies, the chief administrative body for Spanish colonial affairs, took the place of the King and nobles, advised the crown on colonial legislation and served as an appellate court for decisions by Spanish commercial interests.[8] It became the model of all colonial organizations and even in the nineteenth and twentieth centuries, the governments of former Spanish colonies in South America were staffed by the same mercantilist players – lawyers, nobles and old colonial hands – who kept creating organizations based on the colonial models. These organizations were awash in red tape and invariably adopted special regulations when problems arose, an approach that guaranteed plenty of work for lawyers and lawmakers.

Mercantilism's Long Reach

Mercantilism may be thought of as a doctrine followed by a collection of economic policies designed to keep the state strong and prosperous through extensive economic regulation and rigid bureaucracy. Countries with mercantile economies applied very strict rules on foreign trade; aimed at ensuring that the country exported more than it imported. Merchants and governments benefited greatly from this system, which restricted foreign competition and protected domestic monopolies, while it brought high tariffs into the public treasury.

Adam Smith challenged this philosophy in his 1776 work *The Wealth of Nations*, charging that mercantilism created massive economic inefficiencies and benefited producers at the expense of consumers. Smith offered a radically different notion that wealth consists of all the goods that all members of a society consume, a modern and very democratic concept that was starkly at odds with the mercantilist model. John Locke and David Hume also challenged mercantilism in their own writings. But it was in the mercantilist era when Europeans first appeared in the New World, and their colonies tended to copy what existed in Europe.

Institutions, organizations and property rights

To understand fully the problem of informality, its historical roots offer only a starting point. We also need to grasp the fundamental difference between the concepts of institutions and organizations. This difference is essential as it allows for a proper evaluation of informality and an identification of any necessary changes to institutions or organizations to overcome the problem. Whereas poorly defined institutions can create informality, this is not necessarily the case when organizations are malfunctioning. However, the two concepts are usually confounded, especially by those charged with fixing one or the other.

Institutions are the natural dynamics of society. They are a set of rules, norms and traditions, some written and some not, some formal and some informal. Institutions "structure incentives in human exchange, whether political, social or economic."[9] In other words, they hold together and protect the social contract[10] by enforcing contracts and laws and providing a sense of certainty in human exchange. As Nobel laureate economic historian Douglass C. North explains, institutions "are the rules of the game in society or, more formally, are the humanly devised constraints that shape human interaction."[11] Formal institutions can be, but not always, written; they are found in laws – such as the Constitution, Civil Code – and regulations, contracts and administrative procedures. Conversely, informal institutions can be described as norms and values commonly accepted by society, including behavioral expectations. Organizations, while related to institutions, are the tools through which institutions function, sometimes smoothly and sometimes poorly. They can be agencies, ministries, departments. In human terms, they are the actors that pursue common objectives shaped by institutions.

We find a simple illustration of the difference between the two in the area of justice, which is an institution that encompasses the written and unwritten rules, informal traditions and incentives that define just behavior and conflict resolution. By contrast, a government's Ministry of Justice, Judiciary and Courts charged with applying laws are organizations.

Formal markets are guided by institutional structures that establish and ensure a kind of partnership between citizens and the state through which resources are allocated efficiently and transactions are secured, thus reducing uncertainty. All citizens in such markets ought to enjoy the right to share in the resulting benefits from institutions, including social cohesion and profits. The main type of institution is property rights;[12] that is, the right to possess, enjoy and use any asset, including land, movable property, and proprietary ideas to mention a few. The smooth functioning of a formal market depends on the ways in which property rights are defined, applied and enforced.

In this book, one type of property figures prominently – real estate. It is an area where policymakers frequently collapse the notions of institutions and organizations. Property is often viewed simply as land, housing, or shelter with a narrow, specific use, rather than a fully tradable asset with potentially multiple economic and financial uses that increase its value. As a legal term, "real estate" typically encompasses land and anything affixed to it, such as buildings. One may own a home or have money invested in an office or apartment building that rents to tenants. "Real property" is usually distinguished from personal or movable property, such as books or machinery. In countries governed by common law, the terms "real estate" and "real property" are typically used, while countries governed by civil law usually refer to "immovable property."

At first, informal markets might not appear to be part of an institutional structure because of a tendency to associate "institutions" with "formal" rules and structures. In fact, informality stems from the same rules and norms of human behavior represented by formal institutions. Organizations can reinforce informality by the way they apply formal rules of institutions. While in theory, the institution of property rights allows property rights holders to trade any type of property, many organizations may not fulfill their responsibilities in a way that allows for such rights to be exercised fully. The judiciary, the registry, the patent office or the licensing bureau may all reinforce, perhaps inadvertently, the conditions that perpetuate an informal market. As we shall see later, knowing how to apply the distinction between institutions and organizations is critical to the successful development and implementation of policies that can transform informal markets to formal ones and unlock property values in the process.

Institutions and their organizations ought to reflect society's demands at all times. When they do not, exclusion and informality arise as exchanges take place outside the formal rules and organizations. Formal institutions and the organizations associated with them are rarely flexible enough to adapt to the informal norms of behavior, refusing even to recognize informal social and market conduct. Ironically, this exclusion perpetuates informal behavior and further exclusion. Separate sets of rules, formal and informal, create two economic and social languages in the same country.

"Unreal Estate"

Sadly, the situation faced by people forced to conduct their transactions in informal markets suggests that their property is anything but "real." In a very true sense, their assets are locked and to the degree that these people own any property, it might be called unreal estate.

The queen who cannot get a formal bank loan illustrates the problem brilliantly. "La Reina de la Papa" ("The Potato Queen"), a 45-year-old Peruvian potato merchant, lives in a ramshackle settlement on the outskirts of Lima, Peru. Famous throughout her neighborhood for her commercial acumen, the business she runs from her home, a clearinghouse for local potato producers, is a flourishing one. She also imports potatoes from neighboring Bolivia when the local crop is in short supply. La Reina manages potato distribution to many open-air markets that crowd Peru's city squares, playing a vital role in helping to ensure a steady supply of a staple of the Peruvian diet. Her outstanding business network has earned her a healthy profit and considerable respect.

Although clearly she is alive and well – albeit less aristocratic than her title might imply – La Reina does not appear as a business or property owner in any of the official records of Peru, leaving her almost no recourse to leverage her assets. She faces volatility and cash flow challenges and she is unable to expand operations to meet growing market demand, or hedge her business because she cannot formally pledge future earnings or assets – for example, her home and warehouse – as collateral.

La Reina's predicament is neither an accident nor the result of an oversight. No one forgot to include her business in the official records. There is no bureaucratic bottleneck. Her paperwork was not lost somewhere in a pile of records or pending registrations. The problem for La Reina is that she does not formally exist. In a sense, both her real estate and business are "unreal." She is forced to operate in a marketplace of informality where citizens – whether consumers, sellers or investors – are excluded from the formal institutional structures and organizations that presumably exist for their benefit.

Under different circumstances, perhaps in another market or in a different country, La Reina could walk into a bank, meet with a loan officer and secure a line of credit to expand her business. A loan, with her business or home pledged as collateral, could fund a new warehouse that would allow her to break into other markets she has yet to conquer. But she does not have that option because she operates in an environment of informality that is not structurally friendly to markets and growth. Nor is her case unique. Her small business is typical of most that form the backbone of the Peruvian economy: run by individuals or families in their homes or shops on a volatile, short-term cash basis. Her predicament demonstrates the immense obstacles to even simple business development in Peru and elsewhere, and has implications for the country's ability to expand its middle class and secure a stable economic and political future.

Transforming the "Unreal" to Real

People in the developed and developing world face problems similar to those of La Reina. The confusion between institutions and organizations, and the ambiguity or absence of formal property rights are universal. This book tells the story of how a series of institutional changes in Peru successfully transformed "unreal estate" into real estate. The transformation began with a full understanding of how and why institutions had evolved, and then succeeded by overcoming the limitations of traditional corrective approaches that had been used to establish a market based on property. While Peru has its own idiosyncrasies, the story could have unfolded anywhere.

Two elements – institutions and organizations – are essential to understanding and solving the "unreal estate" problem. Two important concepts must follow. Policymakers must see institutions as they are: rules that define and guide socioeconomic human behavior. And, they must see organizations and agencies as tools to implement those rules, not as ends in themselves.

This book will show that transforming unreal assets to real ones offers opportunities to all parties involved – the state, citizens, and investors – provided they have an appropriate vision and can take a long-term view and position. The coming chapters will identify the necessary elements for a successful transformation from the "unreal" to the real, and present the ingredients and strategy of such action.

2
Policy and Politics of Land and Property

Your land is your honor.

— old Arabic saying.

Land hosts us and confines us. It defines our communities and our nations. It is a source of honor and pride. We trace our origins to the land where we were born – our "tierra," our "patrie," our *"patrida,"* our homeland, a place we revere. It gives us identity – we are "from" someplace. Some people obtain their status from their land, adding "von" and "de" to their names, the often aristocratic titles denoting connections to their lineage and estate. Land is both a social reference and a source of wealth, reflecting its ability to be enveloping, enduring and productive, yet scarce and finite, requiring care and attention.

Land's central role in society and the economy is apparent throughout history. Empires and later nation-states based their strength, growth and internal societal status on land concentration and distribution among their classes and subjects. The Roman Empire used land to reward trusted soldiers in retirement, for instance. Those who fought well for the emperor's glory in defending and expanding the empire's territory were given land upon retirement. Much later, wars and revolutions, notably in France and Russia, were fought over land and the right to appropriate the fruits of one's own labor on that asset.

Economists since Adam Smith have recognized that land, together with labor, is one of the main factors of economic production. During the Industrial Revolution, the introduction of technology helped transform land into capital and created a much broader and deeper property-based market.

Today, land remains a significant factor in individual wealth, and people continue to be acutely sensitive to rules for distributing, using and controlling land and property, as well as the ways in which the State appropriates and regulates land. It is the right to property that defines the social and economic exchange of land.

For the homeowner, his property represents a part of his identity, a welcoming retreat from the world, a place to gather with family and friends, and perhaps even a sign of his social status, wealth and place in the community – all intangible elements derived from the value of owning property. These intangible attributes form a part of the basic working principle of a mortgage, a principle that provides a powerful expression of how people value land and property. The mortgage is based not only on the market value of the property but on the fact that the value the borrower places on the property exceeds that of the loan. Lenders assume that no matter how hard-pressed a borrower is, he will do everything in his power to avoid falling behind on mortgage payments, which could lead to foreclosure. This intangible value is the basis of mortgage finance: the lender's belief that the possibility of default is minimal. However, mortgage lending generally only works smoothly in well-functioning markets with low transaction costs.

Philosophers have given considerable attention to exploring human behavior toward land and property. Their work has had a major impact on how land ownership and the institution of property rights are viewed today. John Locke, Jean-Jacques Rousseau, Jeremy Bentham, Thomas Hobbes, John Stuart Mill, David Hume, Karl Marx, Thorstein Veblen and a host of other western thinkers well into the twentieth century devoted themselves to questions of how individuals, communities and the state view property ownership and how those views affect economic and social transactions. Over time, the myriad of ideas developed by these thinkers became reduced rather simplistically to two main concepts: *individual* and *communal* ownership. The English philosopher Locke, and the Swiss-French philosopher Rousseau, express these two opposite perspectives. Locke asserted that land has individual utility and can be accumulated. His *Second Treatise on Government*, published in 1690, stated:

> *As much land as a man tills, plants, improves, cultivates, and can use the product of, so much is his property.*

Rousseau took exception to that notion 72 years later, suggesting that property was a common good and that its accumulation ought to be controlled by the state. In *The Social Contract* (1762), he wrote:

> *The right which each individual has to his own estate is always subordinate to the right which the community has over all ... The general will alone can direct the State according to the object for which it was instituted, i.e., the common good.*

From these two seemingly opposing views, modern ideologies evolved to offer different meanings for land and ownership, as well as different interpretations of its private, public or social function. Marxism, often said to have its roots in Rousseau's thinking, promotes, in the "commune," the concept of equitable land distribution.

The ideology of unfettered capitalism, often linked to Locke, holds that individual wealth spurs the economy and advocates unrestricted private land holding as a way to increase economic growth. Despite appearances, the two views are not *necessarily* diametrically opposed, and can be applied as complementary systems. In fact, the concept of zoning – the public regulation of land and buildings that controls their use – stems from the effort to reconcile the interests represented by these two positions. Specifically, zoning allows for individual use and appropriation of property within a common agreement by a city regarding what type of property use can take place in which area.

From the time of Locke and Rousseau until the middle of the twentieth century there was a largely unbroken view that the institution of property rights and the organizations that ensured the effectiveness of those rights were a significant part of a nation's growth, making it a subject worthy of attention. The subject remains no less important now. Chapter 1 explained that today, much of the key asset of land and property is held outside the formal institutional structures of markets. This means that property is illiquid and people cannot easily use it to secure capital. This raises a series of compelling questions. How did something as important as land become hostage to informal behavior? What social and economic forces led to this? Was it circumstantial? The answers require us to explore the history of countries' institutions, some of which are homegrown and others not. We will see the role of history as well as how both the private and public sectors got involved.

Adopting or creating institutions?

We defined *institutions* as a set of norms and traditions, some written and some not, and some formal and some informal. A country's history largely determines the way in which a country defines its institutions. Institutions are expected to reflect the social contract and to develop symbiotically with the demands of the society they represent. When this development is interrupted, institutions can become stuck in a sort of "time warp," or become inflexible, making them dysfunctional, creating exclusion and informality. In this case, institutions no longer correspond to that societal demand. Why does any of this matter? There are strong indications that economic growth and market efficiency depend on having well-functioning, long-lasting institutions.[1] Countries with such "healthy institutions"[2] have better economic development than countries that have only good macroeconomic policies, a privileged geographical location, or both.[3] Countries that have experienced profound disruptions in the development of their formal institutions, which define their legal and political ruling patterns, have far greater problems in economic growth than countries whose development is uninterrupted, or countries that succeed in adapting new institutions to their communities' existing ones.[4]

The example of southeastern Europe is notable. Beginning in the mid-fifteenth century, the Ottoman Empire began to rule regions that had been part of the Byzantine Empire or that had been under the rule of various kingdoms, encompassing areas that later became Albania, Bulgaria, Greece, Romania and Serbia, to name a few. The Ottoman rulers recognized that the way communities managed land-use and production was central to peace and prosperity and that uprisings were almost certain to result if the peasantry was dissatisfied with the rules for using land and dividing crops.

Meanwhile, Western Europe, after several centuries and a few revolutions, changed its ruling patterns, moving away from empires to nation states in the nineteenth century. The Western Continent developed basic codes of law to reflect the new social contract, framing social and economic behavior in each particular country. The French Civil Code of 1804 became a model for the German Civil Code, as well as for Italy and other newly emerging nations on the continent. As this process unfolded in Western Europe, the regions still ruled by the Ottoman Empire continued operating with their own set of formal rules and administrative structures.

The waning of the Ottoman Empire starting in the early 1800s and culminating in its final dissolution in 1922, left behind a set of new countries with a mix of formal and informal institutions and a gap in political administration. Some institutions were remnants of the Byzantine Empire that had ended in 1453; others were left over from monarchies, mixed with formal institutions established during the Ottoman rule. These newly founded independent "nations" asked for help from "experienced" Western countries. These emerging nations were looking not just for advice but to adopt Western European rules of law. This behavior was spurred in large measure by the fact that the members of the intelligentsia of these new states often had just returned from self-imposed exile in the very countries which they now used as a role model for reform.

In the case of Greece, the country did not only adopt a new set of rules, based on the French and German Civil Code (which both originate from the Napoleonic legal tradition) but in the early 1,800s, even "imported" a king from Bavaria to establish itself as a constitutional monarchy and to become a modern nation state. Other countries, for example Romania and Bulgaria, took similar paths including the adoption of monarchs from Western Europe. All these countries that basically emerged on paper almost overnight wanted independence above everything and gave little thought to whether the written institutions they imported were appropriate for their particular societies. Not surprisingly, their institutions evolved unevenly and in a way that sowed the seeds of future problems.

Does it sound familiar to what happened near the end of the twentieth century in Eastern Europe? After the Cold War, newly independent republics of the former Soviet Union and former Eastern bloc nations looked to the West for advice and rushed to adopt Western legal institutions and organizations, such as civil codes, land and bankruptcy statutes, while setting up a judicial machinery for effective law enforcement. A situation that added to the mosaic of almost 75 years of institutional tradition under communist rule, mixed with the institutions of previous empires and some family-ruled republics in Central and East Asia, such as Kazakhstan. Out came a patchwork quilt, as the social fabric was "interrupted" so many times. The pertinent question is: Did all formal rules that were adopted fit the market demands and social needs of each new country? It appears not and not surprisingly, many of the same countries now are calling for institutional reforms as part of an effort to make their economies more stable.

Similar *breaks* in the formal institutional development of a country are evident in former colonies, where formal institutions typically were left over from their old "mother countries," which established them to cater to their needs. In Latin America and some parts of East Asia, for example, the organizations related to property rights were based on objectives similar to those of organizations of its Spanish and Portuguese colonizers.

The evolution of economic and social institutions over the centuries is central to the subject of this book, but the period from the end of World War II is of particular importance to the understanding of the current situation.

After the war, the Bretton Woods agreement established the International Monetary Fund (IMF) and the International Bank for Reconstruction, which later became the International Bank for Reconstruction and Development (IBRD), and ultimately, the World Bank Group as we know it today. The role of the former was to oversee international financial stability and to provide international liquidity while that of the latter was first to help reconstruct countries devastated by the war and, later, to design economic development policy and undertake projects in developing countries.[5]

Decision makers were cognizant of the fact that well-functioning institutions, including property rights, were important for robust economic growth. However, the unfortunate reality is that there was little attention to reforms targeting those issues, except in Japan, and later in a few other Asian nations. Western Europe already had a well-functioning tradition of the rule of law so that economic intervention – and therefore *development* policy – was narrowly focused on building or rebuilding industry and infrastructure.

Why Japan? After the Japanese aggression during the war, Western allies wanted to ensure that it would not happen again. Part of the solution was US support for land reform in an effort to resolve severe food shortages and soothe mounting social discontent. After the war, Japan's rural economy was still largely feudal; it was essentially a country of tenant farmers. The country faced starvation as imports had stopped and agricultural production was critically damaged.[6] It was obvious to the United States that Japanese written institutions defining the rights to property and asset-related contracts had to change. In order to create incentives for farmers to become more productive, the United States Administration supported new laws that reflected the needs of farmers. US policymakers believed that if Japan had a more participatory economy, the Japanese people would have one less reason to go to war again.[7]

After Imperial Japan surrendered in 1945, US General Douglas MacArthur became the Supreme Commander of the Allied Powers and was charged with rebuilding occupied Japan. As part of that effort, he ordered and supervised a massive land reform.[8] The aim was to change the tenancy system and incentives to give people in Japan a stake in their own labor and savings, which would encourage them to play a more active role in the country's economy, rather than passively following their leaders. This, in turn, would decrease the power of the Japanese elite – still seen as hostile to the United States and to the West.

It was a drastic agricultural reform commonly referred to as agrarian reform. MacArthur was well aware of Japan's landlords, who had successfully diluted efforts to reform property rights since the 1920s,[9] so to counter their opposition, US-ordered reforms took place under the slogan of enhanced food production.[10] Even MacArthur's incisive critics had to admit that land reform in Japan was the most successful achievement of the US occupation policy.[11] The number of individual landowners in Japan increased dramatically, from 31 percent in 1941 to 70 percent in 1955. The percentage of landless tenant farmers declined to less than 4 percent of the population during the same period.[12] The changes worked. Landlordism in Japanese agriculture was abolished. As a result of this intervention and other economic measures that followed, Japan enjoyed stable economic development. Indeed, the economy flourished.

Forgotten pieces in the Cold War *chess game*

The *intentional* intervention into Japanese institutional development was an anomaly in the immediate postwar period, when the focus was mainly on infrastructure development. Then, as the Cold War heated up in the 1950s, the United States favored extending land reforms from Japan to Korea and Taiwan, both of which were seen as linchpins in the new geopolitical standoff between the United States and the Soviet Union. In these two Asian countries, the United States "saw reform as a means to weaken a reactionary political class to release resources for growth."[13]

At the same time, another development emerged in the so-called "Third World," as national liberation movements caught fire in Asia, Africa and Latin America. The US and its allies considered these movements linked to the Soviet Union, and as former European colonies won their independence, the US sought to ensure the new governments stayed in the Western orbit. In Latin America, countries already were nominally independent and the national liberation movements – leftist in nature – focused on ending foreign domination. It took some time before Latin America came to be viewed as part of the Cold War chess game, but eventually, the West sought to halt Latin American leftists in their tracks, which sometimes meant partly acceding to their demands for greater economic equity.

Some modest attempts were made to address land distribution and tenure issues through institutional reforms, especially after the Cuban revolution led by Fidel Castro. In March 1961, US President John F. Kennedy proposed the Alliance for Progress – *Alianza para el Progreso* – for Latin America, modeled after the Marshall Plan in post-war Europe. He described the Alliance as "a vast cooperative effort, unparalleled in magnitude and nobility of purpose, to satisfy the basic needs of the American people for homes, work and land, health and schools – *techo, trabajo y tierra, salud y escuela.*"[14] Undoubtedly, his interest in this Alliance grew out of Cold War fears fanned by Castro, who had expropriated foreign-owned sugar plantations in Cuba and had started his own agrarian reform. It was under the same program that the US approved and sponsored the creation of the Inter-American Development Bank and the Organization of American States. These programs brought only modest results in terms of land redistribution; the programs were too small, too under-funded.[15] While the rhetoric was full, the budget was empty![16]

Notably, reforms that were prescribed for Japan and other Asian countries were not offered to Latin America, which itself was largely feudal-like, with landless farmers. There were some important differences, however. Unlike Japan, Latin America was not devastated by war. Another key difference was that Latin America's elite already had a favorable view of the West, and the "very weight of landed elites in the body politic constituted an obstacle to land reform."[17] Institutional change in that region would have meant altering the status quo, which could create discontent or even animosity on the part of Latin American leaders towards the US and other western allies. No one dispatched MacArthur.

A segmented world

Throughout the Cold War, as development policies focused on individual segments of an economy, they relied on discrete disciplines. A new category of tech-nocrats appeared during this era, versed in the disciplines of economics, planning, management and engineering. These highly-trained individuals were instrumental in shaping the public sector bureaucracies of their countries and colonies, in designing strategic plans for infra-structure development and in establishing international

development agencies.[18] This is also the era when segmentation in policy and investment became increasingly prominent. At the same time, the world was
divided by sharp distinctions between left and right,
capitalist and communist, coloring aid and assistance.
Subjects with direct links to the formal representation
of the social contract, such as the design of rules, contracts and so forth, became "politically sensitive" topics;
as a result institutions and especially the rules that
defined property rights became loaded with "ideology."

It is not surprising that these same technocrats, along
with investors and international development agencies,
soon learned to avoid those sensitive political topics.
Development organizations decided it was sensible to stay
away from anything that involved redefining rules (institutions). Private project financing and development projects typically would consist of large scale investments to
construct highways, roads, power plants, irrigation systems, schools and hospitals. Investment projects are
designed to help a country build its "bricks and mortar"
infrastructure, but there was little emphasis on the institutional and organizational incentives needed to ensure
that governments or stakeholders would sustain such projects after completion. In fact, many governments often
could not maintain the completed infrastructure without
taking on a heavy debt burden.

In the case of real property, rural *or* urban, any intervention would be handled only in a sanitized way. The
idea was to strip away all ideology and politics, avoid
touching any "rules," and steer clear of any controversy
at all costs. There was a fear of getting involved with
changes that might promote either private individual
ownership or communal land that would be state owned
and controlled. That reluctance meant minimal or no
involvement in defining property rights, ownership
arrangements, laws or any other formal institutional

"Fixing" Problems Sometimes Creates New Ones

Governments that try to fix socioeconomic problems often end up creating new ones. Policies starting in the 1960s that led to public housing projects in US inner cities are a telling example. Indirect subsidies, rent control, restrictions on property transfer and other policies were meant to expand affordable housing to meet growing demand by low-income populations, mostly minorities and immigrants. Yet these same housing policies eliminated incentives for homeowners and renters to make improvements or investments and increased risks for investors, resulting in devalued areas and properties.

Housing policies in Peru in the 1960s and 1970s created their own set of problems. The government was faced with a daunting challenge of massive migration as Peruvians flocked from the countryside to Lima, and it responded with entirely new urban neighborhoods. One of these, Villa El Salvador, established by the leftist military government as part of Lima's urban expansion zone in 1972, today is home to some 600,000 people and often is called Latin America's largest shantytown.

Policies such as those that lead to the creation of Villa El Salvador were very much ad hoc. There was little systematic approach to urban population growth; instead, the government chose to create a new place for people to live rather than fix the institutional problems and incentives that made it impossible for Peruvians to establish new, formal communities on their own, based on the existing rules – their rights to use or rent or own property – which would have been a long-term, sustainable solution.

---

structures. Involvement was limited to "technical" activities, for instance, using survey engineers to produce maps and cadastres,[19] creating low-income housing to replace slums and offering financial valuation techniques to aid taxation. Later, in the 1980s, development agencies supported very limited efforts to help in titling but again left rules untouched.

Many western economists and policymakers, throughout the 70s and 80s applied the prevailing view of economic growth at the time, which focused on policies of self-reliance and development of industry and infrastructure.[20] None of these types of policies and projects addressed the overarching issue of institutions and whether they worked or were appropriate in the given countries. In a sense, these policies treated symptoms rather than the disease – an approach also popular in many rich countries. And, as if ignoring institutions were not bad enough, countries' policy responses to demographic changes, for instance migration, often created *additional* problems the existing institutional structures could not handle, making things worse and often increasing informality.

By the 1980s, the governments in many developing countries – particularly in Latin America and Africa – had created unmanageable bureaucracies and debts. The oil crisis in the early 1970s added to most countries' fiscal burdens. These governments were not always financially accountable for the services they provided or the goods produced in state-owned enterprises. Deficits continued to grow, productivity rates declined and inflation erupted into hyperinflation, reaching and exceeding rates of 1,000 percent per month in Peru![21]

The continuous battle with untamed inflation, systematic reform reversals and the Latin American debt crisis of the late 1980s strengthened the need of macroeconomic stability, which became the prevailing model in economic growth and development later in the decade. However, many governments headed by populist politicians continued to adopt ineffective economic policies and could not stick to macroeconomic discipline. They became unwieldy and their fiscal irresponsibility meant a constant battle with growing debts and deficits, which made it impossible for them to borrow and avoid default. These governments' reputational equilibrium was severely damaged, because their behavior was marked by opportunism: the cost of breaking the agreement to honor their debts was perceived to be low. The short-term gains seemed larger than the long-term costs. Economists describe the "original sin" of countries that have a history of this phenomenon – a phenomenon that destroys reputation with effects in the financial markets. Over time, these countries signal to the financial markets incapacity to maintain macroeconomic and fiscal discipline, which prevents them from short- and long-term borrowing abroad or even in their own countries, in domestic currency.[22] For "sinners," policy fixes for their economic fundamentals and current practices matter less than their history and reputation.

Absent fiscal discipline, public policy in these countries became hostage to political agendas. Trust in governments declined in the face of entitlements, inefficiencies and corruption. These countries' reputation in capital markets sank – a situation that only got worse with the Latin debt crisis and the emergence of new, shaky transition economies in the former Soviet bloc.

When economists gathered in the late 1980s to brainstorm a "solution," they prescribed more fiscal discipline, privatization, financial sector reform, and trade liberalization independence, all designed to decrease debt and foster direct foreign investment and growth, an approach, which came to be known as the "Washington Consensus."[23] This consensus became the guide for development policy. Its primary focus was to restore countries' reputations by restructuring their economies. Tools that were used included operations of structural adjustment[24] in order to avoid the destabilization wrought by inflation and uncontrollable debt of the previous decade.

Financial institutions and international development organizations endorsed and pushed these reforms. The debt crisis had threatened the solvency of major commercial banks so they welcomed *any* reforms that would put an end to the "drama" and bring fiscal discipline to these countries. Debt control, debt restructuring through Brady Bonds,[25] currency boards[26] and massive privatization all were seen as signals that these countries were serious about macroeconomic policy changes.

This set of prescriptions was quite effective. For example, in Latin America, hyperinflation was relegated into history, replaced by the kind of single-digit inflation seen in European countries in the late 1990s. Monetary discipline, central bank autonomy, tight fiscal controls and fixed exchange rates finally allowed countries like Argentina, Mexico and Peru to send the right signals to the capital markets. Former "sinners" were redeeming themselves and attracted capital flows and foreign investment. Seeing these countries begin to repay their for-

---

Successes of the Washington Consensus

Even the most obstinate proponents of the "Washington Consensus" have to acknowledge that today the term – justifiably or not[27] – has largely been discredited in the international development debate. This legacy makes it difficult to discuss successes of the 1990s reform policies – but they exist! Hyperinflation in many Latin American countries was tamed through exchange-rate based stabilization plans, for example Argentina brought down inflation from 3,000 percent in 1989 to 3.4 percent in 1994, Mexico and Brazil decreased inflation from 160 percent in 1987 to less than 20 percent in 1991 [Mexico] and 2,000 percent in 1994 to 2 percent in 1998 [Brazil] respectively.[28] At the same time, the trend of negative economic growth that existed in the 1980s (minus 0.6 percent real GDP per capita) was reversed to average growth rates of 2.5 percent between 1991 and 1997.[29]

In Eastern Europe, too, macroeconomic stabilization allowed for economic recovery. In 1997, Bulgaria successfully employed a currency board which tied the local currency to the deutsche mark and now the Euro. This reform arguably helped overcome a banking crisis and significantly decreased inflation rates (from 2,040 percent in 1997 to 1 percent in 1998).[30] While Albania – which we will study in more detail in Chapter 6 – offers an illustrative example of the early successes of macroeconomic stabilization, the country's socioeconomic turmoil after the collapse of the pyramid schemes also reveals the shortcomings of this narrow reform approach. In fact, a main weakness of structural adjustment has been the lack of parallel or subsequent reforms aligning and strengthening the countries' institutional structure, so that it could absorb a collapse like the one in Albania. In this respect, structural adjustment provided a foundation which was insufficiently utilized as institutional reforms were not fully applied to consolidate the early successes of the Washington Consensus.

eign debts spelled success; they were reintegrated into the world economy.

Macroeconomic reform was not enough

These successes showed that macroeconomic policies could work when applied correctly and followed seriously. These reforms typically require top-down decision-making and prescriptive laws that can be implemented quickly, with limited need for input or approval from stakeholders in different organizations. Negotiations entail only a few people, such as the president or prime minister of each country, the heads of the Treasury and the Central Bank, and the economic and finance ministers, simplifying debate. Thus, it is not uncommon for these reforms to take effect with little public attention. Their success very much depends on political commitment and the State's resolve not to reverse its position. However, there were obvious shortcomings: the countries that took the road of macroeconomic reform still suffered from severe income inequality. These deeper problems stemmed from the lack of appropriate institutions, such as a well-functioning judiciary, effective contract and property rights enforcement, effective public service, and so on. In the mid-1990s, some influential thinkers, led by Moises Naim, current editor of Foreign Policy magazine, identified the urgent need to sustain structural adjustment with institutional reforms called "second-generation reforms."[31]

In practice, second-generation, or institutional reforms presented a considerable challenge as policymakers had no map to point the way and no experience to draw upon. Economists and development practitioners at organizations such as the World Bank and the Inter-American Development Bank consistently reported that development agencies lacked the experience in identifying those institutional issues, let alone the experience in handling such reforms. They had to find a way to make wide-reaching societal changes that were a far cry from the usual "top-down" macroeconomic reforms such as maintaining tight monetary policies and fiscal discipline. Many policy experts, as well as country leaders, were skeptical that institutional changes could be made successfully, presenting a significant challenge for those economic development practitioners who sought to make second-generation reforms a priority.

In my own experience beginning in 1991, the suggestion to include institutional reforms in a development program would almost always provoke negative reactions from fellow economists and other colleagues. The safer path was to work on familiar ground, such as reducing government involvement in the economy and markets to minimize distortions and bring about macroeconomic stability.

Neoclassical economics at the time reinforced this view. Economists and policymakers who subscribed to the neoclassical school of thought attributed institutional problems to ineffective and large government. In this view, smaller government is better government; thus, these policymakers favor shrinking government and reducing government interference in and controls on investment and growth. It is no surprise therefore, that in practice, they would recommend organizations reorganize, downsize or privatize, rather than endorse a more comprehensive approach that recognizes the need for economies to have effective formal institutions.

Overlooking institutional issues was no solution, however. Neoclassical economists have recently started to accept the fact that institutions matter and now search for ways to further elaborate on how they fit in economic growth.[32] The need for an appropriate rule of law to ensure contract enforcement, minimize corruption and protect property rights was growing, especially as markets opened, privatization increased and government controls diminished. As countries increasingly requested assistance with institutional issues, the World Bank, International Monetary Fund and other members of the international financial system gradually began to let go of some of their reluctance to address institutions. They started to see that institutions matter in modern markets.[33] However, while a *limited* recognition of the importance of institutions emerged, the gulf between this recognition and actual practice has yet to be fully bridged, in part because there is little knowledge of *how* to fix the problem. Mistakes and stifled reforms continue because the organizations responsible for development were in general not built to address such problems and have grown over time to be even more segmented.

The limits of what we had to work with

It is worth taking some time to explain the forces at play that led technocrats and development practitioners to overlook institutions. According to the neoclassical model, people are rational, independent participants in the market. Institutions are viewed as existing to reduce uncertainty in human exchange and to lower the costs of transactions and production. Provided that government does not intervene and distort the flow of information necessary for trading and setting prices, markets should operate rationally and reach equilibrium – efficiently – at all times. Equilibrium and market efficiency are achieved when transactions are costless.

In the real world, this view has important shortcomings, however, as summarized so well by Nobel Laureate economist Ronald Coase. He pointed out that in the neoclassical model, the overarching assumption is not only that institutions are designed to achieve efficient outcomes, but that they can be ignored in economic analysis precisely because they play no independent role in economic performance.[34] This is one reason neoclassical economists and those who have been traditionally educated in technocratic disciplines, such as lawyers, engineers and administrators have resisted the idea that poorly functioning institutions actually *create* market failures.

Ignorance of institutions and their role is but one shortcoming of this traditional model. Another is that too many professionals seem to ignore the long and difficult histories in their own developed countries that gave rise to strong, healthy institutions. Institutions evolve dynamically. The process is lengthy. Those who were present at the outset pass away, leaving little memory to tell the tale of their experience. Without drawing on the history, explanations of *how* institutional structures were erected, what the underlying incentives were and *what* people thought about them at the time are scarce.

Formal and informal rules have a life. They grow and mature slowly. It is difficult to document anything about institutions as they evolve. Just as a passenger in a train does not see it moving, but only experiences that it *may* be moving, someone involved with an institution may not realize its progression at any given time. But that is not all. When we meet a train at the station, how much thought do we give to the full history of its journey? In fact, we give scant thought to where it started, how many stops it made, and whether there were any major disruptions along the way. If we do not experience something directly, we rarely think about it. With respect to institutions, the modern technocrats "know" institutions when they are already established and functioning, whether well or not. They were not there when the institutions began and they do not experience them "in motion."

When the *history* of institutions is ignored, practition-ers discount the reality of how much time and effort is required to reform institutional structures. It is very difficult to understand how informality is created. They see the extensive problems associated with informality as mere wrinkles to iron out, with no substantive policy implications.

Looking backward before going forward

History, however, has a profound impact on the shap-ing of institutions. We see this, for instance, in the rules of law adopted by any given country. The legal tradi-tion has shaped national approaches to property law, which provides for the enforcement and protection of property rights, while the degree of State intervention in the economy is influenced by legal tradition as well as by political institutions.

There are two major legal traditions in the world: common law and civil law. The English common law of real property gradually evolved to protect private prop-erty owners from the whims of the Crown and the gov-ernment. The Civil Code of France, commonly referred to as the Napoleon Code, also was geared to protect landowners, but in contrast to English common law, it

---

"Civil" and "Common": An Important Distinction

The distinction between *civil* law and *common* law is an important one and figures prominently throughout this book. More detail is in order. Civil law is the legal tradition, derived from Roman law, in which code is used to settle disputes. The emergence of the nation-state in the nine-teenth century gave way to the codification of Roman law and customary law, so that the backbone of modern civil law systems is found in codes, legislation and administrative regulations.

"Civil" and "Common": An Important Distinction – *continued*

In contrast, the common law tradition that prevails in Britain and former British colonies is found in precedents created over time by judicial decisions. The term "common law" also is used to mean the traditional, precedent-based element in the law of any common-law jurisdiction, as opposed to its statutory law or legislation. The term common law derives from medieval England, where the law was administered by the King's courts, making it "common" throughout the realm, as opposed to the local custom applied in manorial or local courts.

Broadly speaking, the common law tradition prevails in the United States and Canada except in Louisiana and Quebec, where French and Spanish legal institutions played a prominent role. Civil law is prevalent on the European continent, in former European colonies, including most of Latin America, and in other countries that have adopted Western legal systems, such as Japan. A legal tradition that came "packaged" in codes was more accessible and easy to import than the English common law based on a multiplicity of judicial precedents.

was inspired by an ideology in which the State is the central player in defining economic and social transactions, including the mechanisms of dispute resolution and enforcement of contracts. Thus, the adoption of a civil code is very much linked to the concept of nation-state and these nations tend to place more emphasis on the rights of the nation-state than on the individual owner.

Resistance to Change from the "Old Guard"

The "old guard" represents vested interest groups that emerge over time and that benefit from confusing and oblique processes. The more transactions costs there are, and the more convoluted the system, the more they benefit. These groups have an interest in perpetuating the bottlenecks that further increase costs. In fact, they become the *guardians* of these systems, making themselves indispensable as the system grows more complicated. These groups usually include members of the legal profession, including lawyers and public notaries, and specific technical experts. Particularly in

Resistance to Change from the "Old Guard"
– *continued*

the civil law tradition, public notaries are a major "old guard" force that is reluctant to change traditional formal institutional patterns. In most civil law jurisdictions, the office of the public notary has a level of prestige and authority unknown in common law countries. Notaries typically enjoy a professional monopoly or quasi-monopoly in the supervision and closing of real estate transactions.

Traditional professional monopolies are reinforced by a trend in post-Cold War education to promote segmentation and technocratic knowledge, often times leading to policy suggestions based on a strict interpretation of the law that is largely unfriendly to the market. A legal professional educated in the classical canons of civil code interpretation, the so-called "lawyer of traditional training," tends to look at the law as a set of fixed rules and principles, rather than as a flexible tool whose main purpose is to facilitate commercial transactions. These lawyers of "traditional training," while advising policymakers and drafting legislation, typically resist changes that would alter some rituals firmly entrenched in the civil law tradition, such as the notion that land transactions should be strictly scrutinized because land, as a resource and a right, is so valuable that trading it would depreciate its social and economic value. This resistance to legal change, and the failure of the legal system to adapt to society's changing demands, is in large measure responsible for the encouragement and expansion of informal practices.

Resistance also comes from those who make their living from the complexity, obliqueness and enormous transactions costs of traditional institutions such as the "transaction middle men" – the *tramitadores*, as well as from those who deliberately corrupt the system, which is easier under informality.

Effective institutional reform requires considering how laws were established and the historical context in which they have evolved. This analysis produces reforms that are appropriate, increasing the odds of success. It also helps reformers identify which groups will resist change, and gauge the level of resistance they are likely to offer. When formal institutions (laws, written rules) are ill defined or dysfunctional over a long period, any attempt to change them will provoke strong resistance from those who have a vested interest in maintaining the status quo.

Reality Check Analysis

Much more often than not, institutional reform is not addressed in practice. Instead, it is "organizational reform" that is undertaken, resulting in many internal restructurings, internal management changes and measures that focus on making organizations more efficient in meeting their original mission and goals. The problem with this approach is that making the organization more efficient may still not serve the interests of the community and society. Ironically, this very approach may be taken by those bent on helping countries through what are commonly known as "capacity building" programs. Genuine reform requires more; to get the correct diagnosis of the problem, there needs to be understanding of informality, why the specific organizations exist and how they work. Achieving a complete diagnosis requires an analytical tool I call Reality Check Analysis, described in this book.

It was the sociologist Max Weber who explained that organizational bureaucracies over time tend to grow separately from the rest of society and are unable to keep up with society's rapid changes.[35] Bureaucracies tend to suffer from "organizational lag," that it, they become rigid and inward-looking, creating a gap between the services they provide and the changing market demand. Ultimately, organizational lag results in organizations that are no longer serving their original purpose but their *own* internal interests. Organizational reform – reshuffling and streamlining the bureaucracy in what is commonly called "reorganization" – often aims to restore organizational integrity and return it to its original mandate or bring it up to date by introducing accountability, performance budgeting, monitoring mechanisms, "scorecard" grading, anti-corruption clauses and ethical standards.

Reform of this sort, however, may be inadequate because the underlying issue – the organization's *very existence* – has not been addressed. What is missing is a look at history and an analysis of the incentives that were in place when the organization was built. Questions that get to the *heart* of the matter are not posed: When the formal institutions (written rules) were established did they reflect what people and markets needed at the time? How have the institutions and their associated organizations changed over time? How have they accommodated the changes in the demands of the people they are supposed to serve? Is a specific organization necessary for the provision of the public good or service in question? Does the organization delineate, enforce and protect the institution of property rights? These are fundamental questions that constitute the backbone of Reality Check Analysis (Figure 2.1).

The analysis starts from where we are now and juxtapose the situation to what happened to the written rules and organizations at each point in time, especially during major shocks in the historical development of a country or market. Keeping in mind very clearly the distinction between institutions and organizations allows us to diagnose correctly the causes of the problem and thus determine an appropriate solution.

The analysis may point out that formal institutions which – at the time of their inception – might have served all or part of society's needs no longer do so. Institutions may have broadened or, as we see most often, may no longer serve *any* of society's needs. Other rules, especially formal rules, may be imported, imposed or adapted in ways that aren't appropriate for the local reality. Asking the right questions is as important as getting the right answers.

Too often, reformers conclude that when organizations aren't working correctly, this is due to a failure to keep up

■ Identify and isolate the problem

■ What are the relevant institutions and organizations?

■ Check institutions throughout history

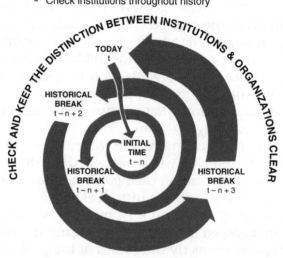

■ Have institutions met societal and market demands over time?

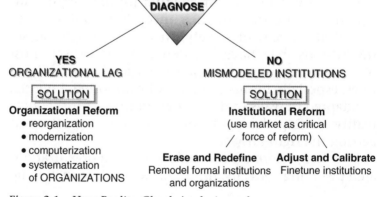

Figure 2.1   How Reality Check Analysis works

with changes – a sort of "organizational lag." Thus, the response to a problem with the justice system, for instance, often is to "reform the judiciary." The absence of formal property rights becomes an issue of land tenure in general terms, which in turn leads to issuing titles, mapping plots and "reforming" the responsible titling authorities.

These approaches ignore the totality of the problems. Reality Check Analysis incorporates a rigorous and what we call *holistic* analysis of the history of a country's political economy, including when, how and why its institutions were built. In most cases, we need to look across sectors and organizations to pinpoint problems and stress points. Examination of disruptions in the country's history, such as colonization or civil war, which may have affected the rules of human interaction and exchange, is central to the methodology used in Reality Check Analysis. It leads to the appropriate diagnosis of the institutional problem by asking the right questions, and then builds on it in developing the necessary solution.

How Institutions Change: An Example from Greece

Empires, wars, occupations, revolutions, antiquity, Greeks, Romans, Byzantines, Turks – all mark the story of Ismini's family property just outside Athens at the port of Avlis, where the coalition of ancient Greeks under the leadership of King Agamemnon, later joined by Achilles, launched a thousand ships to rescue Helen from the Trojans. It is the very people who passed through this land and the history they made that fills Ismini with pride. She is proud of being from Greece, *Hellas*, her *patrida*. Yet, she does not realize that it is this same history that led her to a judicial ordeal that began in 2003 and continued as of this writing. Ismini is in court trying to prove that *her* property, passed on to her from her father and grandfather is actually hers and not the property of someone else who lays claim to it.

How Institutions Change: An Example from Greece – *continued*

Several rules were applied in transferring Ismini's land, originally purchased by her forefathers in the late 1880s from the Ottoman Turks under Ottoman Law using contracts that were based on the laws of newly established Free Greece. These land exchanges involved parties from different countries and legal jurisdictions. The negotiations produced a formal and legitimate contract that corresponded to the needs of the people at the time. The contract provided rights of ownership, and detailed legal boundaries and was registered in the Greek registry of real property called *Ypothicofilakio*.

What was sufficient then seems insufficient now. In 1990, a trespasser decided to declare part of Ismini's property as his own through a contract also registered in the *Ypothicofilakio*. This unresolved, ad hoc claim has created uncertainty and devalued Ismini's property. Chapter 3 provides further detail on how someone can claim property he clearly does not "own." Suffice it to say here that when the property rights system is inadequate, honest misunderstandings and fraud are possible.

Reality Check Analysis is a break with traditional binomial thinking – right/wrong, left/right, private/public, formal/informal, legal/illegal, urban/rural, their culture/ our culture – in favor of a more holistic method. It goes back to the basics and identifies the institutional structure *beyond* the involvement of a single organization. It analyzes land as a resource and as an asset, and checks the rules and norms that have defined the legal structure for land ownership and usage. It compares rural and urban differences, explores property as a public or private good, and considers the incentives that have shaped the institution. It examines the historical patterns of property ownership and any interruptions in that pattern. In essence, it tracks the full history of the institutional structure (formal rules, norms, etc.). In doing so, it uncovers why informality is so pervasive and makes it possible to tailor a solution that is appropriate for the specific environment.

Why does informality matter? A disturbingly large percentage of the world's population lives in a condition of informality, where their property rights are effectively no rights at all as they cannot be formally enforced.[36] In Chapter 3, we explore how this situation has come to pass, explain the elements that constitute formal property rights, and illustrate why all of society benefits when those rights are secure.

3
Tipping Points

> *The world of the Tipping Point is a place where the unexpected becomes expected where the radical change is more than a possibility. It is – contrary to all our expectations – a certainty.*
>
> – Malcolm Gladwell

The legal difficulties confronting Ismini, introduced in Chapter 2, are a telling example of what happens to individuals and their communities when property rights are not secure. Ismini inherited a small property in Greece which her family acquired before 1891. Her ancestors had been among the people who originally purchased the fertile valley and forest lands, home to ancient Avlis, from the Ottoman Turks. Property in this community is quite valuable because of the lushness of the land, its cultural and historical heritage, and its proximity to Athens and the Aegean coastline.

For decades, the community's population was stable and it ran smoothly. Over the generations, despite occasional travels for holidays or business, community members always would return to tend their land. People respected each other and community decisions reflected a balance of common and individual needs.

In Ismini's case, her family's property ownership has formal and legal standing through a bill of sale registered at the *Ypothikofilakio*, Greece's real property registry. There are also topographical surveys, known as physical cadastre, dating from 1890 on file with the local farmer's union, which are indexed by the owners' names, with the associated land parcel shown on the map. The title history and transfers, beginning with the original purchase, are all on record.

Over the years, the community has expanded to include outsiders, brought in by business or marriages, who live alongside the children and grandchildren of the original property owners. Many newcomers have bought property themselves as younger members of the community moved to nearby cities to seek different career opportunities. This movement modified the community's social contract, that is, the relationship of individuals with each other and with respect to their society. Reputation, trust and respect, which once formed the social fabric of Ismini's community, have been stretched thin.

Long ago, Ismini's father granted one of his neighbors a right of passage through his land to the closest road, making it easier for the neighbor to get to his farms. At that time, helping each other was what community members were expected to do. The agreement was a verbal one and wasn't intended to transfer this piece of land to the neighbor. Things changed in 1990 when the neighbor's family, which included some newcomers, wrote a "contract" to "sell" this bit of land to the grandson. The grandson took this contract to the registry and registered "ownership" of land in his own name, adding this plot to his family's original land. The irony is that this manipulative land grab did not set off any red lights at the registry or anywhere else under the formal property system in place in Greece.

Manipulating "rules" that were ineffective and practically unenforceable, these heirs, encouraged by the newcomers in their family, staked their claim in 1994, after both of Ismini's parents and elderly uncles had passed away. The role of newcomers in a community is discussed in some detail below and explains how preexisting formal institutions and organizations may fall short when community rules change. In Ismini's case, informality created the conditions that pit neighbor against neighbor. Ismini finds herself in a bind because if she wished to sell *her* property, the neighbors, with little effort, have created a legal confusion that effectively reduces the property's exchange value.

How could the neighbor "sell" land that did not belong to him? He took advantage of a weak formal property rights system. When the neighbor's grandson took his contract to the local registry, the system in place did not flag the fact that the same plot was owned by someone else and registered in her name. You may ask how that can be.

Although a registry system exists in Greece, – established in 1850 by a law based directly on the French legal tradition – it appears insufficient for today's market demands. Indeed, the country has begun an effort to modernize the system, which functions largely as archives of documents that usually are not cross-referenced and looks more like a deeds registry. Most records are archived by the owner's name, in alphabetical order, rather than by address, and do not provide a legal reference to a topographical map. The system is beset by transactions costs. For example, property buyers and sellers have to bear extra costs as only lawyers are allowed to do title searches required for sales and other real estate transfers. All searches must be done manually at the regional registry, which may involve checking decades-old materials. The task is daunting, costly and often does not provide adequate security for enforcing property rights, especially for estates, peripheral urban properties or farm lands because it is based on a loose description of "meets and bounds." This method describes in prose the boundaries of a particular parcel of land, based on physical features of the local geography, along with directions and distances.[1]

The community's institution (rules) of property rights, once based on trust and reputation, is no longer suitable to its needs as the community is changing. The country's *institutions* and *organizations* have not been well-suited for the task, either. The result: Ismini faces multitude of legal hurdles to secure her rights to land that the family clearly bought paid for and has maintained for more than 100 years.

Trust makes property rights reliable

Ismini's story is, in part, one of weakening social capital, with loss of trust and thus reliability in enforcing property rights. To understand how important social capital is to secure property rights, it is necessary first to define the term. "Social capital" typically comprises the attitudes, spirit and willingness that people bring to their collective civic activities. It is measured as the degree to which a community or society cooperates and collaborates through a variety of mechanisms, including shared trust, norms, values and social networks. Much has been written about social capital and it has puzzled policy practitioners because finding ways to foster or reconstitute it have proven to be a challenge.

Trust is at the center of social capital. It is the institutional norm that defines the social contract –social and economic agreements of a community governing ownership, use and disposal of assets. These agreements are enforceable because they are based on the reputations of the parties involved and the mutual trust that flows from those reputations. In fact, trust is the underlying condition that keeps reputations intact.

Why Does Social Capital Matter?

The term "social capital"[2] is used to describe the relationships and norms that define a society's social interactions; it essentially refers to the value of social networks. If societies can draw on a high level of trust, cooperation, and solidarity, transaction costs are believed to be reduced. In this respect, social capital is critical for societies to prosper.

Why does social capital matter? According to Putnam, social capital – which creates a sense of *belonging* – helps citizens resolve collective problems more easily, clears a path for communities to advance smoothly, and widens awareness of the many ways in which our fates are linked. There is considerable evidence that communities with a high level of social capital are more likely to benefit from lower crime figures, better health, higher educational attainment and stronger economic growth.

In his book *Trust*,[3] Francis Fukuyama discusses how trust can be the cause and effect of market development. Fukuyama suggests that trust – a key element of social capital – is a cultural product of society, incited by economists and other policymakers. Social capital ebbs and flows. When trust and belonging are in decline, or have been harmed, policymakers face the practical challenge of how to restore or improve social capital. There is no consensus on what to do under such circumstances, but most scholars agree that resources must be concentrated first on the more intractable problems that arise when social capital deteriorates.

Countries' formal written rules that do not rely on reputation and mutual trust are seen by citizens as *alien* to the social contract and even illegitimate. They may in fact have no real effect on the community. Citizens will tend to operate under their own common arrangements, separate from the formal ones. It is this persistent division that is seen and labeled as "informality."

The centrality of trust is obvious in a so-called "handshake" culture. The handshake represents an agreement between two parties, enforceable based solely on trust. It puts the reputations of the parties at stake. In a small community, where the same people repeatedly do business with each other – engaging in what game theorists call repetitive cooperative games[4] – the motivation to honor the handshake is that there is only one or, at most, two chances to break an agreement and maintain a good reputation. In short order, broken handshakes create bad reputations, with little chance to recover, creating an incentive to honor those deals.

As long as a community is confined and stable, contracts will be complied with, or enforced, because of reputation and trust. The incentives are clear. However, the traditional way of doing business often changes radically when a significant number of newcomers are introduced to a once confined and stable community. The newcomers bring their own disparate new rules and ideas which clash with the old ones that are slowly ignored. The cohesion represented by the very same trust that once made the community and its social and economic transactions function begins to disintegrate.

A critical mass of newcomers can bring this effect to a "tipping point," which in turn breaks the existing trust among community members regarding the *enforcement* of community rules, including property rights.[5] When this tipping point is reached, the community becomes less secure; the new rules create instability because players can start choosing to engage in non-cooperative transactions (games), as reputation is no longer a stabilizer. In an environment in flux between new and old rules, newcomers view the old rules as not applying to them, creating a break in the cohesion represented by the very trust that once made the community and its social and economic transactions function. In such circumstances, where there is little reason to care about long-term trust, people tend to engage in one-shot deals or "games." There is no expectation of dealing (i.e. playing) with the same person again; instead, the objective is to extract the highest return from a single transaction, so opportunism becomes the name of the game. The structure and predictability that community members could once count on disappears. Situations such as the one facing Ismini erupt everywhere. Social capital in the community is progressively thinning.

Faced, therefore, with the inability to use their traditional, informal enforcement mechanisms for transactions, long-time community members feel that they must turn to the formal organizations – the very organizations they have not relied on in the past. It should come as no surprise that they find them insufficient; had these organizations been effective, they would have been more useful previously in fostering secure transactions. We see this same phenomenon in countries where, over long periods of time, layers and layers of rules – formal and informal – and organizations sit one atop the other. These rules and their associated organizations may have been inherited, adopted in time of crisis, or imported from elsewhere. When the community reaches the tipping point and finally puts the preexisting formal rules to the test, players are disappointed because the formal rules do not relate to and cannot cater to present market reality.

When a community or market opens to external influences and the local formal rules are not adequate to properly manage this new reality, it makes sense to ask whether they were designed to manage such reality at any time. When formal rules afford scant protection, the typical results are negative: slow growth, dampened investing and prices, uncertainty, frustration and short-term, opportunistic investing. Markets in such environments are far from robust. They do not expand and they certainly do not show longevity. Financing in such environments tends to be largely on a short-term cash basis rather than longer term asset-based lending. Elements of formality *and* informality compete for primacy in a system that does not work for all.

The case of Ismini is eye opening. Her story shows the wrinkles that exist in the property-based market in her country. We observe a market that is neither fully *informal* nor fully *formal*. There are formal rules aimed at guiding property rights and human behavior, but they do not seem to operate effectively and appear to be a poor substitute for the old informal arrangements. Ismini is caught between the formal and the informal, at the precise point where the informal rules of her community no longer work because the community – having reached the tipping point described earlier – is no longer stable and the old agreements and behaviors, based on mutual respect, have given way to new behaviors that once would have been unacceptable. The formal rules seem alien as they are no substitute for the community's trust – a key element of its *social capital*. The break in trust at the community level is compounded by the break in trust with the State and its formal institutions (rules), because the State is not delivering on its implicit promise of good governance.[6] Nevertheless, Ismini and others in the community have no choice but to turn to the formal rules and organizations, in this case, the courts, to resolve a conflict that would have been handled differently in decades past.

As Ismini fights to enforce her property rights, the market ambiguity over who owns the property and the length of time needed to reach a resolution lowers the property value. Her case isn't unique; other property owners find themselves in similar circumstances because the property rights structure has not kept up with the country's development specifically its macroeconomic development.

This insecurity keeps the market from reaching its full potential because the inherent unpredictability puts off investors. The related problems of weakened social capital and the erosion of trust are not confined to Greece or other advanced industrialized countries. These problems become glaringly obvious when these countries open up their economy to international competition and labor becomes more mobile, giving people the opportunity to get better jobs elsewhere. New openness in trade and greater labor mobility leads to a larger volume of continuous transactions, each one based in part on the transactions that preceded it, and may involve complete strangers from different communities and countries. Such transactions depend a lot more on the security of formal contracts (rights) since those involved in the original transaction are no longer in the picture and old reputations carry no weight.

The mortgage market offers a clear illustration. When Jack, a single working man living in Tampa, Florida, wants to obtain a home mortgage, his reputation matters to the bank that makes the loan. Later, the bank packages Jack's loan with other mortgages to create a security. In that transaction, Jack's personal reputation is no longer of direct consequence. By the time that security and thousands of others are traded on the world's stock exchanges, Jack is no longer relevant, as what matters is the trust and reliability of the formal financial system.

In a world where mortgage derivative instruments change hands and social contracts are undergoing change, the need for secure property rights becomes increasingly important. That requires a system that makes Jack's reputation inconsequential and ensures that Ismini's ownership is respected. It requires a system where trust is the glue for any transaction, which is not based on individuals trusting in one another alone, but on individuals trusting that the system itself will safeguard transactions.

The ingredients of a secure property rights system

Property markets are efficient and yield economic and social benefits when property rights – that is, the rights to own, use and dispose of property – are well defined and enforced. Secure property rights result only from a properly functioning *system* dedicated to maintaining the integrity of those rights, coupled with an effective mechanism to enforce them. They are not the fruit of any one organization, public entity or authority. It is here where we see the *marriage* of institutions and organizations: the operational structure of rules detail how property contracts and transactions will be defined, and structure the mechanisms to make those rights "real."

What should it look like? A formal, secure property rights system requires several key ingredients. First, it is imperative that there be *a credible, formal institutional and organizational structure* that defines how the right will be created. The design of this element, commonly referred to as the "upstream" process of property rights, is mainly a task that generates the right.

The second ingredient is the *flow of information directly from the property rights holders*. This "bottom-up" element, feeds in the upstream process and, is comprised of all the data the rights holders are expected to provide to the formal system at any given time to keep the property rights current and relevant. Together, these two ingredients are interrelated and expected to provide all necessary data into the property rights system at all times. When citizens do not *trust* the State, these two ingredients will not function, even with legal obligations, because people do not engage in formal transactions unless they see a clear benefit.

As policymakers design the first ingredient, they will rely on institutional arrangements, including the rules and laws that define the property market and conflict resolution. They also will look at the organizations, including the agencies and their internal procedures that apply those definitions, such as the registry, courts and titling agencies. They will consider the procedures and requirements for property registration, titling, contracts and so forth; standardize the manner in which information is recorded and establish how data are collected at all levels. In brief, the formal property rights institutions (legal structures) govern how contracts are drafted and executed, establish enforcement of financial contracts and guaranties, define the role of public notaries, lawyers and engineers and set administrative requirements.

The information component requires special attention, because *sufficient information regarding the legal and geographic aspects of each property* is vital. Well-constructed property rights systems must reflect all the information over time about the property and its ownership, and must have built-in incentives for the users to provide this information. This information is the direct input that creates the property right; in fact, absent this input, formal property rights do not exist. The information must be recognized and accepted as legitimate by all concerned. Informality will grow if the mechanisms for providing this information, or the organizations responsible for keeping it are not trusted.

Informality is the direct result of a property rights system that is not trustworthy. The lack of secure property registration, mistaken records in the registry, messy data entry and out-of-date records can all lead to conflicts on paper or in the courts. The result is a system unable to enforce local market transactions, thus suppressing the market and its ability to expand.

The third ingredient of a secure property rights system is *trust in the State and its services*. Trust is what constitutes a genuine *partnership* between the users and the State. This is *the* critical success factor. It is the "make-or-break" ingredient that determines whether all transactions and contracts will be effective. The onus is on the State to *convince* citizens that it can deliver effective governance. The greater the scope of informality and the lower the level of trust, the larger the number of possible market players kept out of the formal market. The litmus test for success is the growth of an actual property-based market that brings in *all* those people who have been operating under informality for *so* many years – often, for generations – and who have been alienated from the market.

Trust is a most challenging ingredient, especially when the changes necessary to establish a properly functioning property rights system step on the toes of special interests. Overcoming that opposition requires a high level of commitment, consistency and tenacity on the State's part. Special interest groups will oppose the changes fiercely. Once a critical mass of users reaps the benefits, a new tipping point is reached – this time, a positive one – which will help solidify changes.

Without these three ingredients – *credible, formal institutions and organizations, correct information and trust* – the security and effective enforcement of property rights is viewed as suspect, and the attendant risk makes the property unmarketable. Formal property rights, in effect, do not exist, and society cannot realize the benefits of smooth and effective social and economic transactions. Instead, resources are wasted and investment cannot reach its full potential.

The importance of a reliable recording system

Property rights represent an asset and make those assets tradable. There can be no property rights unless contracts that convey titles to land and property are enforceable. In most legal systems, the ability to enforce property rights against third parties who did not participate in the transaction requires that those contracts, or the portion purporting to transfer property rights, be made public. It is public registration that makes the information about the asset and the contract public. By making this information available for public inspection at a reasonable cost, risks are mitigated and easier to assess because the law, which is based on a universal agreement concerning the underlying principles of property rights, provides that *"what is not in the registry is not in the world."* Thus, hidden risks or "secret liens" that cannot be ascertained from the public registry cannot be set up against third parties. Public registration makes property rights enforceable, reduces ambiguity, increases incentives to invest, ensures the integrity of the information and the system, and helps to settle disputes. Registration calls for a registry open to public inspection. A properly functioning registry complements the three ingredients: integrity, accessibility and public access of information.

A functioning property registry is indispensable. For property to be traded securely in a formal market context, it requires multiple players who can remain anonymous. There must be a system that can handle the volume of transactions required by the real estate market at any given time and place. Informal rules become formal; only formal rules and entities can provide a consistent level of security and trust from one transaction to the next and consistent information of all kinds – ownership, area, location, liens, risks – on every asset being traded as well as on the participants. A well-functioning property registry makes all this possible.

Why is the information collected and processed by a properly established property rights system so important? By making the information about the right to the asset publicly available, a well-functioning, market-oriented registry transforms the information of a clearly private good, such as a real estate asset, into a public good. Instead of limiting property exchanges to a confined area with a specific number of players, a greater number and variety of exchanges are possible, thus increasing the property's value. The key difference is that all information on the right is indexed and easily available. This decreases asymmetry of information and thereby better enables people to exercise the right to sell, rent or use the property in any way they wish, including as collateral. A registry should provide property holders with indisputable proof of ownership which protects them both from uncertainty and fraud.

Establishing a well-functioning registry can be difficult. In Peru, when we attempted to strip down the reform effort to the essentials, we continually came up against the technocrats and legal experts involved in work on land or property. With their segmented approach, discussed in Chapter 2, they would either overlook the issue of a registry altogether or focus on its *technicalities*. Generally, they would suggest modernizing the registry buildings, and computerizing registration processes. They believed this to be an "easy fix" for whatever problems they agreed existed, while disregarding the issue of land and property *markets*. They considered the problem to be that of organizational lag calling for organizational restructuring when, in fact, it was a deeper issue of institutions. Reality Check Analysis, which uses the proper historical perspective of the problem, would have presented a fitting solution. Of course, since all these efforts only addressed improving internal processes, there was little success in broadening the scope of formal, secure property rights for all citizens. Rather, all the institutional bottlenecks continued and informality, with all its inadequacies, kept expanding.

Socioeconomic benefits

The economic effects of insecure property rights are very serious. On a broader social scale, it leads to prohibitively high-risk assessments, foregone or unsophisticated transactions, low volumes of trade, a low level of information exchange and the absence of innovation. The uncertainty associated with informal property lowers the market value of the asset by reducing the owner's incentive to invest in and improve the asset. It makes the asset a less desirable good, reducing its current and future expected value. This leads to a waste of resources for the government, citizens and investors who partici- pate in the market. Because of the uncertainty of infor- mal ownership, a sort of "tax" is generated, but unlike a typical tax, it is not collected by anyone so its "value" is never captured; it is a permanent loss of well-being to society, what economists call a deadweight loss, or excess burden.[7]

Economists, anthropologists and sociologists who study property rights have identified compelling socioeco- nomic benefits arising from formal property. Looking strictly at financial markets, for instance, property rights formally establish an *increased credit supply and liquidity*, because as information about property is more secure, uncertainty becomes less of an issue. The more that is known about a transaction, the better. It makes it easier for lenders to accurately gauge and manage risk, the uncertainty embedded in *any* trading action or exchange. Trading at low cost makes it possible to apply a lower interest rate based on higher predictability of lending risk.

When risk is lower, loans are more likely to be avail- able to property owners. Imagine the growth that La Reina de la Papa, introduced in Chapter 1, could spur in her small corner of the Peruvian economy if she could secure a formal private-sector loan to expand her busi- ness using her home as collateral. In fact, collateralized lending for the *informales* began in Peru soon after the property rights system underwent reform.

As a system becomes more effective in producing reliable property rights, the wider availability of information reduces *transactions costs*. This information gives market participants the ability to assess the costs of their decisions. For instance, it can help one to assess whether it is best to engage in a transaction now or later, or whether to trade one asset or another. Information is at the center of market transactions because, in one sense, it is the information itself – secure, truthful and complete – that is being traded. Decreasing transactions costs benefits the State, investors and simple loan holders.

Enhanced security, coupled with an improved access to credit, provides financial resources for improving the use and productivity of the property.[8] The greater assurance offered by formal property rights boosts confidence and increases *incentives to make improvements and invest in buildings, equipment, infrastructure and so forth.* I saw this first-hand in 1993 when I visited Huaycan, a new urban settlement on the outskirts of Lima, established to house the large influx of rural Peruvians to the city. I was there as part of a public awareness campaign to explain the benefits and costs of the new registration system represented by *Registro Predial Urbano*, established by the reform detailed in Chapters 4 and 5. The town was dusty and brown from the coastal desert sands. The streets were unpaved. Houses were small. The rooms in most homes, as is typical in new urban settlements, were multipurpose: part of the kitchen or the main room also was used as bedroom, and other rooms had been transformed into a mini-factory for making garments or for some other small-scale commercial activity.

Returning two years later, my team and I were flabbergasted by the changes we saw. Theory had been given flesh and bones and put into practice. The town's transformation was truly incredible. I did not recognize much from my last visit.

The community leader remembered me from my previous visit and proudly offered to show me and my team around. *"We're all so happy with the change,"* she said. *"Let me show you the residential streets – you see, we have small yards now with flowers, and then over there is the commercial area where we moved our businesses."*

In a few short years, Huaycan had become a small, urban village with paved streets and small gardens. It was far from luxurious, but the registered property owners were proud of what they had. They had cleaned and painted their homes, many of which now had second stories, elaborate roofs and additions. Construction was going on everywhere. Kitchens were kitchens for families, and commercial activity took place in a separate part of town dedicated to that purpose. All this had taken place because the residents, once they possessed formal rights, were able to secure the financing to make these improvements.

This transformation was not only obvious in the urban districts; we saw it as well in the agricultural lands. As economists explain quite well, secure property rights do result in a *considerable increase in agricultural productivity*. The fact that transactions costs decrease gives more people the freedom to take part in the market and encourages them to make the best use of their land, which leads to consolidation of land at its optimal size and to its use by the most optimal users.[9]

Huando, a valley in coastal Peru close to Lima, was another example of how formal property rights can transform properties. It had been famous for its citrus production under the ownership of the old *hacienda* families. When it was expropriated and turned into a cooperative in the late 1960s, productivity began to drop and output ultimately plummeted. There was no incentive for private investment, and credit came chiefly from the State in the form of special purpose loans from State owned banks – called development banks – which operated on highly subsidized credit terms (mainly interest rate subsidies low repayment rates). No new technologies were introduced to help the farmers who expected to produce high-quality fruit for domestic and foreign markets. As debts mounted, the cooperative's members felt increasingly cornered. Over time, several left to seek greener pastures elsewhere and the cultivated areas of the cooperative's lands turned close to a jungle of weeds.

When reform unfolded in the early 1990s and private land ownership was reintroduced, the Huando cooperative members decided to break up the cooperative to meet individual and business needs, and register the property in the *Registro Predial Rural*. The institutional reform of property gave them the flexibility to divide their land according to use, set up agri-businesses, and borrow against their asset. Productivity increased significantly[10] and the citrus farmers were able to pay off their debts to the state banks and begin exporting their produce. It is easy to see in these examples how formal property rights *increase property values*.

We also saw in Peru how the secure ownership that comes with formal property rights fosters *greater labor mobility and decreases the likelihood of child labor*.[11] Under the pre-reform system, a farmer who left his farm to pursue an employment opportunity in the city risked having his land confiscated by the government and given to someone who would work the land. Fear of losing one's property if one is not physically present leads urban residents in Peru to work at home in cottage industries, or always keep a family member at home to defend the property. Typically, one spouse would become an unlicensed street vendor, called *"ambulante,"* while the other would remain at home and run an informal business, for example, making furniture or garments often employing children. With a formal system, though, people can defend their property rights legally in a formal institutional setting rather than having to do so physically on site. They are no longer so strictly limited by location when they seek employment.

These are some of the many economic benefits of formal property rights. There are social benefits as well. In general, the greater market power that formal property rights provide individuals allows all income groups to play an increasingly important role in social and economic decision-making. The process of making property rights formal extends the informal social contract that acknowledges people's rights at the community level to formal institutions.

As the example of Huaycan shows, establishing formal property rights helps eliminate the gap between rich and poor and the opportunities available to each, thus *strengthening the middle-class*. This is a direct result of the market power imbued in individuals when they enjoy secure property rights. They have the choice of disposing of their property in the way that is best for them. Their new status gives them new voice. In turn, these people can carve more of a place for themselves in society and play a more active role in social and economic decision-making. A positive result for the country as a whole because it is usually the middle class that benefits from and sustains reforms and development changes.

In Peru, making property rights formal created *equal standing for citizens* and had a particularly beneficial effect for women by establishing shared ownership of property by unmarried couples, a common arrangement known as *"convivencia."* Although shared property ownership under convivencia has always been a constitutional right in Peru, it had not been put into effect under the traditional property laws which followed the old Spanish tradition of awarding title and registration to the man, as head of the family. The property always would be titled and registered in the man's name.

Regardless of gender, race or citizenship, people who own property enjoy the benefits that come with secure property rights, whether the ownership is individual or shared. With a new rights system, those who suffered from discrimination in the past are given the formal means to demand and obtain equal access to credit, justice, inheritance and so on. As we saw in Peru, they are less likely to turn to extra-governmental means to enforce their ownership claims because they have a renewed partnership with the State in an environment of secure transactions. The existence of public records minimizes disputes and indeed prevents them from arising in the first place since ownership can be readily determined. The State's services are no longer exclusively for society's elites, but for everyone. The result is *enhanced social stability*.

Social stability also is enhanced because society has to allocate fewer resources to monitoring and enforcing property rights since the institutional structure is more effective, which helps strengthen a trust-based partnership between the people and their government. Community members volunteer information about their property because they trust it will be used appropriately and to their benefit. The private sector becomes more involved because it trusts the predictability of the business environment.

Of course, governments also benefit from formality. The increased information that comes with formal property rights enables local or central governments, their respective public organizations and even private suppliers of public services to provide *more effective delivery of public services and utilities*, for instance, roads, water, electricity. Further, public agencies and private corporations can *plan resource management more effectively* when there is formal data on property rights. It is easier to *enforce environmental regulations*. When property owners are clearly identified, *revenue collection is more efficient.*

Reform in Peru began by establishing a new system of formal representation of rights to real property that matched the demands of society and the market. It was in Peru where we applied the principles of a registry system to create a robust property market. It was in Peru where we started to apply Reality Check Analysis in order to identify what was wrong with the existing informal process and *why* it had developed in this way. Our aim was to create a system that would provide a formal representation of property, reducing market uncertainty and expanding investment opportunities. Peru afforded the opportunity to test this objective against myriad challenges, including a poor system of incentives, dysfunctional organizations and a legacy of trying every imaginable political ideology and economic system at one time or another through a history of colonization and later independence.

That is the story of Chapter 4.

4
A Transformation Begins

I would like to invite you to my home for a drink and then show you my new warehouse down the road. We no longer work in the same place we live.
– Resident and community leader in Haycan

Peru is one of many countries that have suffered from informality, intransigent institutions and the absence of solid, enforceable property rights that provide citizens with the ability to trade real estate assets in a formal market. Its story will look familiar to other countries with similar problems, and its experience shows how these problems can be addressed and overcome in a way that benefits property owners, investors, lenders and the government.

Part of what makes the case of Peru so interesting is its rich historical legacy, all depicted in its institutions. The mystical stories of the legendary Incas and Macchu Picchu, Tupac Amaru and his battles with the Spaniards, the mysterious Nasca Lines, the beautiful pure gold and silver handmade relics in the churches of Cuzco are all part of Peru's enticing history. Its journey through modern times is painted in the same strong colors of its past, with migrants searching for opportunities in the new world replacing conquistadores and explorers. Peru today is a mosaic of cultures, a melting pot of indigenous people, whites, blacks, Europeans, Chinese, Japanese and Africans, whose art and music are renowned and whose sophisticated cuisine is one of the world's great secrets.[1] During the second half of the twentieth century, Peru struggled to match its past grandeur in so many ways, most obviously through a multitude of economic experiments.

Peru has applied an array of vastly different economic policies over the years. It experimented with autarchy – a policy of economic independence and self-reliance – then a mix of free market policies in the early 1980s, followed by a new era of open market economics in the early 1990s, precipitated by the country defaulting on its international debt. It bridged capitalism and socialism in original ways. It shifted from private ownership to collectivism, to massive nationalizations and back again. It applied varied schools of economic thought in the extreme, resulting in extreme social and economic outcomes. At different times, the country has been a "transitional" economy, a "developing" economy, a closed economy and an attractive destination for foreign direct investment. It is a country renowned for the richness of its natural resources, especially mineral ores – gold, silver and copper – with traditionally important exports in ores, agriculture and fisheries. Today, Peru's economy is once again competing in the world market. This "checkered" history affords a vivid illustration of how Reality Check Analysis can be applied.

The year 1990 marked a new beginning in the nation's modern political economy – a real commitment by a new government to restructure the fundamental macroeconomic conditions. Peru's new leaders were dedicated to rectifying a deteriorating economy suffering from negative economic growth (GDP declined by 11.7 percent in 1989 and 5.1 percent in 1990), hyperinflation (7,485.7

percent in 1990),[2] and weighed down by inefficient, state-owned enterprises that accounted for a significant 15 percent of GDP in 1990.[3] Peru underwent deep changes to instill fiscal discipline and end a long tradition of policy reform reversals, commonly known as U-turns. Peru's focus on macroeconomic adjustment comes as no surprise as this was the time when the Washington Consensus guided the international development debate. The aim of these reforms was to increase reserves and revenues so Peru could begin to pay back its international debt; stabilize the exchange rate; put a halt to hyperinflation; establish inflationary discipline; open the country to trade and foreign capital – in short, establish Peru as a country worth investing in. Attracting investment also called for Peru's government to commit to a regulatory framework that would provide effective and efficient contract enforcement.

Property rights were not on the agenda of Peru's reforms in the early 1990s; in fact, they made the agenda somewhat coincidentally and gained momentum by reconstituting trust and security in the institution of property-related transactions. When the idea of launching property rights reform emerged, it helped that Peru's overall economic reform environment and commitment to change were strong. A set of additional factors, however, were paramount to guaranteeing the success of these reforms: the design of the property rights reform model itself; the commitment to its implementation by key players; tenacity in the face of relentless opposition; and the ability to build partnerships that strengthened and deepened momentum for reform.

The reform effort succeeded because it employed a new method of analysis presented in this book, which directly benefited more than four million Peruvians in less than four years.[4] Peru's property rights reform program, together with macroeconomic adjustment and privatization, has become one of the country's most significant economic policy achievements. The reforms helped correct long-suppressed property prices and introduced more than $4 billion of previously informal real estate assets to the capital markets.[5] It allowed homeowners to obtain credit for construction and investment. Finally, obtaining formal ownership had other benefits too, including giving owners more security about their home and at the same time, more freedom to work and travel outside their homes. The initiative has received international recognition and its design has been designated as a best practice.[6]

The beginning of change

In 1991, I was part of the World Bank's Country Operations Division, which was responsible for assisting Peru, Brazil and Venezuela re-enter international financial markets. The division analyzed the different sectors of these economies, made recommendations for policy reforms, originated Structural Adjustment Loans[7] to support macroeconomic stabilization and coordinated privatization strategy programs. It was the time of so-called first-generation reforms, which were typically done in a "top-down" manner, where agreements were negotiated with top-level decision makers in each country who then implemented policy changes.

Macroeconomic adjustment allowed a country to create an environment for economic growth that would attract foreign investment, mainly through privatizations. Privatization tasks generally look clearcut and Peru was no exception: identify the state-owned enterprises, get agreement to privatize them from the minister of economy and finance, negotiate with labor unions – a tough but manageable task in a relatively weak economy, like Peru –, decide to break up the target companies if appropriate, and then proceed with valuation and pricing.

Yet as the privatization program unfolded in Peru, things became sticky. While the established rules (institutional structures) and responsible entities (organizations) defined *how* companies and entrepreneurs ought to operate, *how* transactions ought to take place and *how* contracts ought to be enforced, we came to an unexpected impasse: the majority of state-owned enterprises and their assets had not been fully recorded in the registry of companies. This rendered their valuation very difficult – especially problematic for commodities such as mineral ores. Again and again, we would bump into this hidden skeleton of institutional decay.

It was surprising to find such a large percentage of an economy handled on an informal basis, especially since the enterprises in question were state-run. Of course, no one doubted the existence of these companies or that they were owned by the government. Had it just been an oversight?

When we looked into addressing the problem by simply registering what was not registered, using the existing laws and regulations as well as the existing registries, we yet hit another wall. We knew what needed to be done – get the companies and assets registered – but the cost under the existing system was prohibitively high and the necessary bureaucratic processes seemed endless. Oblique rules, regulations and laws, an unpredictable number of agencies from which one had to get clearances, and the vast discretion afforded to officials complicated the process and made it obvious that we could not begin to privatize suitably within the existing system. Privatization would require a change in the institutional structures to allow these state-owned companies to be sold to investors and be publicly traded.

It was only logical to ask the obvious: Why were these companies not registered? Reality Check Analysis provided a helpful tool to identify factors which had prevented Peruvians from using the existing registry system. Using this method of analysis, we discovered that an important element of the problem was *distorted incentives*: people did not consider the "benefits" of registration to be worth the trouble. How had this come to pass?

We found that Peru experienced long periods of isolation from the international financial markets, most recently from the late 1960s to the early 1990s. Its basic written institutions (written rules) dated back to the nineteenth century and were heavily influenced by mercantilist ideas. When we helped privatize the principal state-owned enterprises, we found ourselves working with a small economy and a limited number of market players. As companies did not rely on the international capital markets for financing, registration was perceived as an unnecessary formality, a luxury that provided little or no added market value. The rules and organizations, developed for a small and confined society with few transactions were wholly inadequate for what Peru wanted to become: an open economy competing in the international markets.

Best Addresses Aren't Limited to Formal Owners

It is all too common for people to use the dichotomy described in Chapter 2 and divide the world *simplistically* into formal and informal. In this view, *formal* applies to urban centers and "developed countries," and informal is used to describe badly documented rural areas and new urban settlements with distinct names depending on their origin: Argentina's *villas miserias*, Brazil's *favelas*, Chile's *callampas*, Morocco's *bidonvilles*, Peru's *pueblos jovenes* and *tugurios*, the Philippines's *shantytowns*, South Africa's *townships* and Venezuela's *barrios* are only some examples. Those who draw this type of distinction blame informality on "culture," lifestyles, taste and so on.

Best Addresses Aren't Limited to Formal Owners –
continued

Yet informal property owners also are found in affluent city centers
and wealthy suburbs. As parts of New York City, such as Soho or TriBeCa,
or Washington, DC's U Street neighborhood became upscale, the new
residents lived side by side with people "squatting" in old warehouses or
renting slum apartments on a month-to-month basis. Similarly, Ismini's
property in Greece is on a prime location, as is the case for so many hundreds of thousands of Peruvians who live in Lima's Surco or in the posh
neighborhood of Miraflores.

This simplistic view has ramifications: it gets in the way of change and
makes reformers myopic for a problem's true solution.

The registration dilemma wasn't limited to state-owned
enterprises. We found that the majority of assets, especially real property, did not appear in any official records
while existing ownership records were woefully out of
date.

Businesses were only part of Peru's property rights
story. Peruvian workers and farmers were just as affected
by the inadequacies of this system. In 1990, more than
50 percent of property owners were not duly registered.[8]
These properties are called *propiedades informales* and
people residing on them are commonly referred to as
informales.

Peru had undertaken many efforts through the years to
address demographic changes due to sudden and rapid
urban migration. In 1940, only 35 percent of Peru's population was urban; by 1972, some 60 percent of Peruvians
lived in cities.[9] Peru sought to relieve housing shortages,
even at the risk of undermining macroeconomic stability.
It offered subsidized loans for housing and construction,
built low-income housing and promoted creation of some
new urban communities. Government interventions that
set prices and interest rates below market rates or offered
indirect subsidies created unfair competition to private

finance and investment, crowding it out. It was far from a level playing field. Yet little had been done to establish secure property rights, an element that on its own discouraged commercial banks from collateral-based lending.

It became clear that we needed to tackle property rights head-on, transform the informal to formal, and create new markets that would push investment opportunities and economic benefits to a new arena. But this would not be a simple matter of issuing titles or deeds or even restructuring and modernizing existing agencies. Reform would have to change the rules of the game so that property would be transformed into a tradable asset, giving individuals the freedom of *choice* to use what is theirs in ways that best served *their* interests. Peru needed to embark on a massive institutional reform of the very foundation of its property rights system.

To undertake the institutional reform that was necessary, we had to identify what was missing from the existing property rights system to make it functional and effective. Reality Check Analysis, our analytical tool, guided us to the correct diagnosis of the problem and allowed us to create a reform and a strategy tailored for Peru's specific needs.

Getting to the diagnosis

We started our analysis with Peru's property market how it presented itself in the early 1990s, which included studying how the market functioned and how it was affected by the surrounding economic and social reality. We then systematically analyzed how the country's land and property institutions corresponded to Peru's society and its property market at various points in history up to the present. This intensive examination is the core of

Reality Check Analysis, which allowed us to diagnose whether we were faced with "organizational lag" or institutions that had been "inappropriately modeled" from the start. In the case of "organizational lag," the problem would be centered in inefficient and inflexible bureaucracies and organizations, with an unspoken assumption that appropriate institutions were in place. Such diagnosis would call for a thorough restructuring of the internal processes of the organizations in question, which most people would commonly, and incorrectly in my view, understand as "institutional reform." However, if the institutions had been modeled inappropriately from the start, the solution is less obvious. In such cases, the written laws, rules and regulations have failed to represent the demands of society and consequently, the same is true for the corresponding organizations. This diagnosis, which we found ourselves faced within Peru, is more complex to resolve and requires deeper and more extensive reform to align and adjust market forces to reality.

We concluded that fixing the existing organizations would be an easy way out that would not offer a true solution. It would be like patching a tire on a broken wheel. The divide between the country's market reality and its written institutions and organizations had become too deep, while the organizations had taken on a life of their own and were rife with corruption. Instead, we decided to focus on one goal: correct the institutions embodied in written laws, rules and regulations so as to establish a tradable asset base. We helped recast Peru's laws and regulations to reflect the social contract, and built-in flexibility so that the system could adapt to future changes. We decided to establish a new property rights system with new laws and regulations, using two organizations: a modern registry and a new government agency to implement and oversee the reform effort.

Getting closer to reality

As we fashioned a solution for the future, we looked to the past. We studied Peru's Constitution, Civil Code, property laws and financial regulations to understand changes that affected property before and during the republic, during the military dictatorship, and later in the transition to democracy and an open market economy in the 1980s. Then we examined all the organizations related to the property market and how they had evolved and been guided by the written institutions of the State. In the early 1990s, Peru's property market, like much of its economy, was distorted, mainly due to its inappropriately modeled property rights' institutions.

The situation we found was one in which the existing public registry and other government authorities, including municipalities, mapping, titling and tax authorities, *rarely had the correct information* about properties, either because the property rights system did not update information or because there was little incentive for rights "holders" to keep information current or correct mistakes. The overall system and its processes were complex and unpredictable, and requisites, bureaucracies and special interest groups were ubiquitous.

Costs, in fees and time, were exorbitant. For example, an individual wanting to register a contract of sale or a title by the government had to deal with 14 government offices before even getting to the actual registry, and hundreds of steps.[10] It required spending the equivalent of more than US$2,200 dollars and waiting between three to 20 years.[11] If there were conflicts over property, the judiciary represented an additional, expensive delay; it could take seven years or more to resolve a dispute. The problem of *moral hazard* was strongly present. Powerful professional "monopolies" were another impediment that increased costs. In Peru, as in many civil code countries, the Colegio de Notarios set quotas to limit the number of lawyers who could become public notaries. Some civil code lawyers and notaries defended – and, in fact, still defend today – limiting the number of notaries under a "legal security" argument. In the early 1990s, less than 20 notaries

Figure 4.1   Peru's institutions in 1990: a patch-work of historical breaks

served Lima's seven million inhabitants – even though the law required that all asset transactions, including inheritances, purchases, sales, licenses and user permits, as well as family-law transactions, go through a notary!

Accountability and quality controls were absent from public organizations charged with providing services to citizens. Bribery and corruption were often the only way to escape the labyrinth and obtain a registration certificate or resolve a claim, which biased the process in favor of those who could afford to pay bribes.

Peru's inability to efficiently administer a property rights system created uncertainty in the market – as a consequence, the *financial sector saw no opportunity in real estate, only risks.* Prices were distorted, the valuation system was rudimentary. Banks had little interest in holding mortgages.[12] Loans were mainly granted based on a borrower's reputation so that the few properties that *were* mortgaged included agricultural estates and a very few urban homes whose owners were well-known to lenders.

Our analysis allowed us to unveil Peru's past institutional behavior, find out how all this had come to pass, and understand the patch-work of its historical development (see Figure 4.1) factors that could bring a country to such a point.

A "melting pot" that had not quite done the job

Peru began its "Western" life in the early sixteenth century. After several failed attempts by Spain to get to the Incan riches, a small force of Spanish conquistadors arrived in the northern part of the country late in 1531. This invasion started a period of colonial rule which lasted nearly 300 years. In 1821, Peru became a republic and embarked on its journey toward becoming an independent, modern economy.

The Spanish brought their legal and market traditions to the new world. In Continental Europe, the Napoleon Civil Code became the legal model for Peru, as it did for all of Latin America. Rules for trade and individual ownership mimicked those in Europe at the time. Property rights in Peru were well defined, specifying who the legal owner was and detailing topography by "meets and bounds," described in Chapter 3. Properties were registered at the *Registro de la Propiedad Inmueble*, established in 1888.[13] Prior to that, notaries had been the sole record keepers of property transactions.

The direct descendants of Spanish colonizers and other Europeans controlled Peru for much of its history. Their surnames indicated that lineage and were a sort of "guarantee" in social and business engagements. Many went to Britain and France to be educated and moved in Continental social circles. In fact, the Peruvian elite was very much a part of the international "club," and was commonly known as the GCU – *Gente Como Uno*, or "people like oneself." These people shared a European culture of individual ownership and market transactions, in contrast to the communal "ownership" of the indigenous population. Peru's elite were devoted to their feudal-like estates and the social and economic status their properties provided; some also worked in banking and commerce, as is typical in a mercantilist-style economy. These families strongly discouraged social mixing and marriages with the indigenous or black population, or the new immigrants from China and Japan, and these cultural and ethnic distinctions have only softened over time, not disappeared.

Unlike the elite, the indigenous farmers working on *haciendas* were landless – as had been the case long before the Spanish arrived.[14] They had "different language, customs and dress" and "no access to the legal system serving those of European descent."[15] Some have characterized their work conditions as servitude-like. Landless farmers became increasingly conscious of the disparities as the new formal type of society, which felt foreign to them, took shape.

By the 1960s, social discontent was brewing as the income disparity between the haves and the have-nots had grown precipitously, exacerbated by the persistent decline in agricultural productivity. Urban migration soared, requiring more food to come to cities while agricultural production was declining. Farmers came to blame agricultural stagnation on the *hacienda* owners, and the political balance began to shift away from the landed elite. Disgruntled farmers demanded better wages and ultimately, ownership of the land they and their families had been working for generations. Landowners entered the 1960s with the expectation that sooner or later, their properties would be subject to some kind of expropriation, either formally or informally, and they sought to avoid that to the extent they could.[16] Some implemented special rental arrangements to appease the discontent, giving farmers "use" rights to a piece of the land they worked. These farmers, known as *Yanaconas*, would not pay rent to the owner but would receive a portion of the land's production in exchange for their labor.

Open revolt broke out in 1962 in the valleys of La Convencion and Lares, near Cuzco, pitting landless farmers against large landowners – *terrateniente* – and their managers, known as *gamonales*.[17] The peasant uprising was led by Hugo Blanco, a Peruvian contemporary of Che Guevara, who studied agronomy in Argentina, where he became acquainted with the Trotsky movement. Blanco organized peasants in unions against the landowners. The movement was defeated and he was sent to prison in 1963.[18] Peru's ruling elite – through the Peruvian Congress – refused to accede to the farmers' demands or appreciate the gravity of the situation. In 1963, Congress blunted President Belaúnde's agrarian reform, rendering it mostly ineffective.

Amid the persistent social unrest, the country's economic problems intensified and an inflationary spiral began to set in. Peruvian armed forces also grew restless. The military, which supported Belaúnde's election, was unhappy with his handling of the Cuzco insurgency. Matters came to a head in 1968 when the generals decided that the president had sold out the country to the International Petroleum Company in negotiations over US-controlled oil fields in Peru, which the armed forces wanted nationalized. Yet, not fulfilling its promise, the US's "Alliance for Progress" had not delivered effective land reform programs to Peru, or indeed, Latin America.

The stage was set for a military coup, which was welcomed by ordinary Peruvians when it took place on October 3, 1968. A ruling *junta* was formed, and one of its members, General Juan Velasco Alvarado, was named president – a post he held until being ousted in 1975 by another member of the *junta*, General Morales Bermudes, who ruled until 1980, when democracy was restituted with Belaúnde returning to serve as president once more.

Peru's *junta* moved boldly, implementing left wing policies, including a sweeping change in land policy to address the discontent and take from the "haves" and give to the "have-nots." This radical step, known as *The Agrarian Reform*,[19] was very different from any land or agrarian reform attempted in the past and was the only such reform undertaken by a military government in Latin America. It was one of the most far-reaching economic and social experiments that Latin America had experienced.[20] While bold, the junta's policies did not break wholly with the past; in keeping with the times, the policies relied on a segmented approach toward intervention that was laden with ideology.

The 1969 Agrarian Reform's social revolution

The Agrarian Reform aimed at transforming the existing property rights structure in Peru and ultimately affected more than 80 percent of the productive agricultural lands along the coast and in the highlands and communal lands[21] of the rainforest. The urban areas were not immune, as cities had spilled over into the surrounding rural lands in an attempt to accommodate the waves of rural immigrants, first in the urban centers called "*tugurios*" and soon after in "*pueblos jovenes*" at the city's edges.

Many of the problems we faced later came from what the Agrarian Reform did not do. It did not create a *market* for land or real property. Instead, the reform redistributed land to those who had none in an effort to bring about "justice," resolve class differences and quiet the anger and unrest exploited by Hugo Blanco and others. This "social revolution" was undertaken quickly, abruptly, sometimes even violently, with little consideration of finalizing the process legally.

The Agrarian Reform was implemented by the *Dirección General de Reforma Agraria y Asentamiento Rural*, an agency of the Ministry of Agriculture. Its mandate was to redistribute rural and urban property to the landless, individually and collectively. The process entailed three steps. The first, known as "*afectación*," identified properties to seize, exempting landowners holding less than 50 hectares, and main houses on *haciendas*. Next came "*expropiación*," also referred to as "*confiscación*," in which the State bought the previously identified land at a legally established price called "*justiprecio*" – which was, in fact, a negligible amount that did not correspond to the land's market price or the value of any investment the owner had made to the land or property. Finally, with *"realocación"* the State granted expropriated land to individuals or cooperatives. Some 9.5 million hectares previously owned by ten thousand owners were transferred to over 400 thousand families. The holdings represented over 85 percent of all privately held land.[22] All told, the Agrarian Reform expropriated big *haciendas* and created coops and individual properties by issuing an Agrarian Reform Title, which was called the *"Titulo Verde"* or green title.

The Agrarian Reform's underlying principle, inspired by Hugo Blanco, was that the land belonged to whoever worked it: *la tierra pertenece a quien la trabaja*. Land was a social good, not meant to be hoarded or used as a financial investment – a principle that prohibited it from being sold or used as collateral. Transfers could occur only through inheritance or with State approval.

Peru's Constitution at the time reflected these principles very clearly. Farmers could not leave their property

---

Hanging on the Vine: A Snapshot of One Effect of the Agrarian Reform

Tacama, a famous vineyard owned by the Olachea family, is located in Ica's valley, a fertile oasis in Peru's coastal desert. The surrounding area of 2,000 hectares is home to Latin America's oldest vineyards, planted by the Spanish in the sixteenth century. For centuries, it has produced one of the region's finest wines and was one of Peru's most precious jewels.

Productivity began to plummet when most of the land was expropriated under the Agrarian Reform. The new farm policies confused incentives, eliminating the pride of ownership among newly created cooperatives, and production suffered.

When the Agrarian Reform came to an end, the Olachea family repurchased some of the land it originally owned. It amassed a vineyard of only 180 hectares, which is returning to its former productivity. Today, Tacama wine is exported to high-end consumer markets in the United States, Britain and elsewhere. Sour grapes are a thing of the past.

fallow or unattended for more than a few months; if they did, it would be confiscated by the State for redistribution to somebody else in need of land. This made mobility almost impossible and ensured the poor got poorer. It was a vicious circle: farms (*Chacras*) were less productive, so farmers would migrate to the city seeking better opportunities and lose their *chacras* while finding it virtually impossible to get formal rights to their urban home. Ownership of the *chacras* would revert to the State and the land could be turned over to someone who *would* work it. After a specific amount of time, if the "new" farmer could prove to officials of the Ministry of Agriculture that he had worked the land, he would be issued a *"certificado de posesión"*, a certificate of possession, which was only occasionally followed much later by proper Agrarian Reform property title.

It is important to understand the role of the State at the time. Peru's ruling *junta* viewed itself as "The Law" and thus had no need for any administrative details that would formally define the new property rights system, apart from the broad Agrarian Reform law. It created no incentives for those who were "given" land through an Agrarian Reform title to register it. In fact, the State *itself* did not register most of the land *it* expropriated, making the registry an increasingly irrelevant organization.

Over time, the Agrarian Reform issued a few titles to farmers who benefited from the reforms, some of which were registered, and a lot of certificates of possession, an official document that could not be registered because it did not provide a right of ownership or use. Instead, these certificates served as an administrative shortcut, offering an official receipt acknowledging legitimate land use. The Ministry of Agriculture issued these certificates itself, allowing farmers to receive seeds, salaries and subsidies, because the agency implementing the Agrarian

Reform was under the influence of partisan activists who were not concerned with formalities such as issuing the Agrarian Reform titles. Popular demand eventually shifted from requesting "land" to requesting a "title" – a government document that proved the farmers' connection to their land.

Meanwhile, to complicate matters further, certificates of possession and titles issued by the government were not based on information that delineated pencel boundaries or legally defined the user. This made transfers and overlapping claims difficult, costly and very time consuming to resolve. Land trafficking in the urban peripheries created further complications. Some *hacienda* owners, in an effort to avoid having their land expropriated for almost nothing, took part in "under-the-table" land sales to new urban immigrants. None of these sales could be formally registered. The large urban migration legitimized this activity since government policies and programs were unable to absorb the vast numbers of Peruvians moving into the cities.

Peru's government responded to these informal urban property holdings first with absolute repression, then tolerance and finally, by officially accepting them but without going through any institutional change that would introduce these properties to the formal market. In some cases, it even encouraged the creation of some new settlements, but in all cases, Peru's government demanded proof of ownership, and took at least five years[23] before it would officially accept an ownership claim.

Furthermore, government interventions coming from every direction – to address massive urban immigration, declining farm productivity and so on – meant organizations worked at cross-purposes, creating a sort of procedural schizophrenia. None of the "competing" documents they issued – all legal and all involving some important characteristic of the property in question – expressed the fullness of an enduring, formal property right. In fact, there was no real appreciation of the importance of a formal right or its role in creating a proper real estate market – a problem we confronted again and again. As the years went by, all of these documents – Agrarian Reform titles, certificates of possession, private contracts, receipts of transfer and so on – took on lives of their own, leaving the later reform effort of the 1990s to address a vast documentation muddle.

The military regime's policies had other consequences as well, leading the economy into a downward spiral. In the early 1970s, economic policy focused on promoting industry and agricultural self sufficiency. The former reallocated resources to new areas that proved less productive and the Peruvian farm became even more impoverished, accelerating migration to cities. Agricultural output grew by only 0.5 percent annually during the 1970s.[24] Low productivity pushed many cooperatives to break up without government approval. All this increased the level of informality. Pressure for further change mounted as the country's agricultural productivity continued to decline.[25] Agriculture's share of Peru's GDP fell from 22 percent in 1950 to 13 percent in 1970 and to 6 percent in 1990, while almost a third of the labor force was still working in agriculture.

None of the economic policies and measures Peru's leaders tried in the 1970s and after the reestablishment of democracy in the 1980s seemed to work. Trust kept eroding and informality expanded as authorities focused on one "quick fix" after another – import substitution, large housing projects, new, government-created urban settlements such as Villa El Salvador and Huaycan, handouts to farmers, cooperatives, nationalizations and partial privatization. Each step only reinforced an entitlement mentality – a policy of the State playing a paternalistic role. Peru appeared doomed to remain a dysfunctional, less-developed country. It was a fertile environment for further unrest.

A new kind of "protection"

Peru's problems deepened. By 1980, it was under attack by two well-organized, radical far-left rebel movements, *Sendero Luminoso* (Shining Path) and *Movimiento Revolucionario Tupac Amaru* – MRTA – (Revolutionary Movement of Tupac Amaru.) *Sendero* followed a Maoist ideology while MRTA was Cuban inspired. Rural and urban Peruvians, including residents of the new urban settlements, found themselves hosting and even joining these armed guerilla groups. Both groups served as a kind of alternative government, claiming to provide services – especially security – where the State had

---

The Appeal of the Alternative

The absence of property rights can have serious repercussions for the social fabric of a country. Many argue that it results in mostly poor informal owners having only a weak connection to the formal government. The lack of governance and legitimacy of the rule of law encourages the creation of alternative governance groups, perhaps even the emergence of terrorist movements. *Sendero Luminoso* and MRTA built their political strength precisely by projecting themselves as alternative providers of governance who would protect the poorer classes' properties and interests.

The grip of these radical groups and their anti-government sentiment was slow to fade. In the late 1990s, a colleague and I were visiting a new urban settlement, the first time in years that outsiders were able to travel to that area, which had been a stronghold for the revolutionaries. We saw red graffiti on a wall that read "reformers are not patriots" and "the government is a traitor," reflecting *Senderismo*, the ideology associated with *Sendero Luminoso*. We asked our host, who was the community's leader, whether there were a lot of *Senderistas* in the settlement. At first, she seemed surprised by the question. Her answer was shocking: "Well, we all have been *Senderistas* at some time."

fallen short. Among other things, *Sendero Luminoso* and MRTA "protected" and "enforced" property rights in the areas they controlled.

There was nothing benevolent about these movements, however, which aimed to supplant the government by force and manipulation. Peru suffered a civil war for nearly 20 years that cost anywhere from 25,000 to 70,000 lives, depending on who is doing the counting.[26] Private investment was another casualty – it became very difficult and costly as investors had to provide security for themselves and their families, as well as for their investments. At the time, it was almost impossible to enjoy the local architecture; all properties worth seeing were surrounded by very tall, thick walls and private police.

Taking advantage of a new opportunity for change

The new leadership that came to power in 1990 shocked the Peruvian elite and the world. Alberto Fujimori, a descendent of Japanese immigrants, won Peru's presidential election, defeating Mario Vargas Llosa, an internationally acclaimed Peruvian literary author. Fujimori, an engineer and university professor, and clearly not a GCU, had no international backing and seemed to have no concrete political agenda. He was determined to reestablish Peru's competitive position in the world by expanding and modernizing the economy, and to respond to the demands of a divided and distrusting population operating in both the informal and formal economic structures.

Peru's economic and social situation did not look promising as Fujimori took office. Confidence was low. Citizens had lost their trust in the State, political leaders, parties and anything that represented the status quo. Peru – neither a fully planned nor a completely free market economy – was going through a confused period of transition, with its institutional structures clearly out of order. It was attracting only modest interest from world capital markets. Most market transactions were local, cash-based and immediate. Entitlements were running rampant. Credit was not part of the financial game. The government's economic policies, which attempted to fix Peru's problems, wound up being reversed. In the late 1980s, this practice spurred hyperinflation, exorbitant foreign indebtedness, informality and – finally – default.

Peru's situation was very similar to that in countries that have out-of-whack economic fundamentals and are unable to control their country risk, thus scaring off foreign investment.[27] Many of these countries get in a worse situation when ineffective institutions fail to serve as catalysts in the economy. In Peru, the institutions were not responsive to the demands of the society and were too rigid to anticipate or accommodate changes coming from the shocks of political or economic interventions, for example. The country's *existing institutions were not up to the task*, leaving in place social divisions and inefficient markets that could not effectively enforce property rights and contracts.

Drinking Chicha Was Not Enough

The loss of trust was palpable. I saw it when I traveled outside Lima with officials from the Ministry of Agriculture to meet and talk with farmers, typically on Saturdays, when people would be at home enjoying their day off. After hours of listening to stories, eating and drinking *chicha*, a fiery homemade, corn-based alcoholic drink, I would ask farmers about their future and how secure they felt about their property. When I asked if they had proof of ownership, titles or any certificates, they would turn cautious, defensive and dismissive all at once, and did not want to entertain my questions. Since I was accompanied by government officials, they thought I was one as well, and might use any information against them. No amount of drinking could make us partners.

The dense and twisted institutional structure that arose over time created a series of breakdowns in the partnership between Peruvians and their State. The many botched attempts to mend that partnership shattered trust further, weakening and in many cases, breaking this partnership.

Uncertainty in Peru's property market in the early 1990s was the convoluted legacy of the 1969 Agrarian Reform and all the history that preceded it. Our research had found original hacienda owners who were still registered as such despite having their land expropriated. We came across many cases where expropriations had been contested in court, yet the claims had never been enforced. We frequently found cases of overlapping actions taken by various government authorities to give ownership or usage titles for the same land to multiple beneficiaries.

That so many "legal" titles had been issued on the same plot of land by different politicians and state agencies was the ultimate betrayal. Such papers had very little market value. The effect was similar to what occurs when governments try to meet demand for rising wages in populist fashion – printing more money, which in turn makes all money less valuable. Peru's property muddle, ironically all legal, made it hard to know "officially" or "formally" who was the actual owner and title holder, the size of the plot and other essential information about a piece of property.

For those who wanted formal registered titles, we found the bureaucratic journey they had to navigate to be excruciating. Organizations involved in defining property rights – the registry, titling authorities and the courts – cared little for their clients and were unaccountable for their services. Meanwhile, each new government policy put into effect would add confusion and create more steps in the journey to register a property.

Further questions lead to best design

The result was utter bedlam. Institutional goals were not clear and the organizations had become more and more bureaucratic, overlapping and increasingly irrelevant. The existing registration system, more than a century old, had registered very few properties, leaving the vast majority of urban and rural properties outside the formal market. We needed to find a way to quickly introduce a critical mass of formal property rights to jump-start the new market in Peru. We calculated that one million properties were needed, which meant that the system had to be able to process thousands of property transactions a day.[28] We wondered if the existing system, including the registry, could adjust to effectively handle a growing and more sophisticated property market. How we designed the reform was going to be decisive.

We asked more questions and focused on identifying challenges that our reform plan would need to address. One challenge was to break the cycle of codependency between citizens and the State, where the State felt it had an obligation to directly provide everything to citizens who expected the State would always be there to meet their requests. This codependency resulted in the gov-ernment adopting paternalistic policies, rather than build an "enabling environment" that would create the conditions for economic growth. Moreover, high transactions costs, oblique processes, information asymmetry and moral hazard behavior had created all sorts of corruption, both intentional and unintentional. The *tramitadores*, or middle-men described in Chapter 1, had livelihoods that depended on a poorly functioning system. It was the same for notaries, who deemed transactions to be legal only with their involvement. Other professionals such as survey engineers, topographers, lawyers and architects preyed on poor and middle-class informal owners who longed to achieve formal status through their property holdings, perhaps by acquiring a title. These professionals profited from the systemic confusion, hiring themselves out ostensibly to facilitate final approval of a title or registration, often making quick cash without ever producing results.

Most important, however, we needed to know when the right time was to introduce reform. Should it be *before* macroeconomic adjustment? After the economy stabilized? If so, how long after? If we agreed instead that it was best to do first- and second-generation reforms in parallel, how would that work? Should we tackle the entire country at once? The sooner we could answer these questions, the sooner Peru's property owners and investors in and outside the country would benefit from the changes we proposed. An additional challenge was the fact that institutional reforms were not widely considered at the time we started this reform process. Most thinkers did not start recognizing it and writing about it until the mid-1990s, and it was not on the list of policy options. The World Bank, for example, had not formally embraced such attempts and did not consider them part of the core business of the organization, so there was little support for those who advocated such changes.

We also needed to know how to create partnerships with government officials and political parties that would champion the changes. How would we address their political fears? How would we establish market momentum that would make reforms self-sustaining? The importance of these partnerships is described in Chapter 5, and the strategic questions that arise in any institutional reform effort are discussed more generally in Chapter 6.

Drawing the solution

As we looked at restructuring Peru's institutions to reflect the reality of the country, we touched on sore points of the past. The Agrarian Reform Law and its related regulations remained the official institution guiding land and property transactions, although some privatizations had occurred, officially and unofficially, and a new registry, called *Registro Predial*, was established in 1988 based on legal advice and research by the Institute for Liberty and Democracy, headed by Hernando de Soto. It was only in the early 1990s, the Agrarian Reform Law was rescinded and Peru's new Constitution expressly permitted individual land ownership and sales. It was not until the mid-1990s that Peru's government agreed to undertake a thorough, nationwide property rights reform, aimed at creating security and efficient asset tradability.

We therefore still *worked* with the earlier rectifying efforts in 1997, and since we needed to dramatically reduce transactions costs, we saw no choice but to eliminate functions of the 14 agencies that were involved in property rights processing. In their place, we envisioned an effective registration system built around the still very small, new registry, and operating under the umbrella of the Commission for the Formalization of Informal Property, or Cofopri, which would be responsible for implementing and fine-tuning institutional changes.

The new registry was designed to be a self-sustaining, profit-making center, giving citizens it served a voice in claiming rights to their assets. We introduced accountability in the system's processes, striving in essence to create a public structure that operated with private-sector efficiency. We also introduced an administrative dispute resolution process as an alternative to excruciating lengthy court proceedings.

Because the new system was voluntary, we had to assess citizens' willingness to participate, so we began by examining the degree to which people wanted formal property ownership. We found that people were eager to obtain a formal claim to their property, which many had sought for years. We followed with a public awareness campaign to introduce people to the benefits and potential costs of formal property rights, and to answer questions they had. We found that Peruvians were so used to a broken system that they distrusted what was offered to them and had endless questions. Lastly, we undertook the job of transforming informal property owners to formal ones by collecting and verifying information about the owner and the property.

The reform unfolded in stages, from a regional pilot to a nationwide program. Each stage increased the number of formal rights holders and the number and variety of property transactions, transforming the real estate market into a deeper, more liquid one – demonstrating that the changes were working. We used these successes to thwart the considerable opposition we faced and eventually extend reforms nationwide.

The first stage, starting in the early 1990s, was a pilot program with the new registry aiming to secure formal property rights for owners that the traditional registry had not served. The support received at this early stage, from those in and out of government, was pivotal. The proposal for the pilot was the work of Carlos Boloña, then Peru's minister of economy and finance, and was endorsed and approved by Armeane Choksi, then World Bank director for Peru, Brazil and Venezuela. The World Bank helped with bilateral grant funding.

The results were significant. In the pilot, approximately 88,000 registrations, mostly in urban areas, were added to the new registry, *Registro Predial*. The new property rights regime that emerged engendered trust. By removing barri-

---

Breaking a Bad Mold and Moving to an Appropriate Property Rights System

The new property rights system gave the vast majority of Peruvians access to the benefits of property registration. Unlike the traditional system, the new one offered continually updated information and registration on a large scale, allowing new, formal owners to participate in formal market transactions and the State to become a better manager of real estate information.

The modern system has a number of advantages over the traditional one. In addition to covering a much larger database, the modern system is accessible and transparent to all. Registrations are based on clear requirements outlined in the new laws and regulations. Employees have specific roles and are held accountable to their supervisors as well as to their customers. The system relies on continuous feedback from users, making it sustainable because the citizenry is largely responsible for input and quality control.

After the new system developed an index of more than a million registrations, the traditional registry had to change and connect its operations with the modern system, something we considered a great success.

---

ers to entry, making registration more accessible, decentralizing it and involving property owners, the new system pushed towards an end to informality. The new market players created by this system were the key to the shift from informal to formal ownership and to releasing the locked-up value of assets. At the end of the pilot in late 1993, the new registry's success underscored just how inadequate the old institutional structure had been.[29]

Not surprisingly, the pilot did not give us a full definition of the reform design. Informality had been around for a long time in Peru and was hiding behind all sorts of institutional bottlenecks that were not all obvious at first glance. We kept uncovering more informality – including misspellings and discrepancies in documents, or conflicting zoning regulations – and transactions costs that interfered with the goal of achieving a liquid property market. The key, therefore, was to establish broad reform that would be flexible enough to allow for any adjustments needed along the way.

Special interests seek to undermine reform

As the reform was gaining acceptance among Peruvians and the modern registry expanded its market base, opposition was jelling among special interest groups desperate to save the old system on which they relied. Debate over the speed, legal security and shape of reform became highly politicized. Influential, politically connected opponents sowed confusion about the reforms and banded together to influence policymakers *against* change. Reform opponents used the initial geographic limitations of the pilot to undermine its validity and sought to contain its impact going forward, preventing a nationwide expansion.

Technocrats joined in the opposition out of distrust of a reform that had little to do with the usual narrowly focused projects of survey engineering, mapping and computer technology.

Lawyers and legal professionals of traditional training in and outside Peru – some at development organizations, even some at the World Bank – would dismiss or oppose the changes, claiming that they were unconstitutional. These professionals opposed transforming "unreal estate" to ownership of real property, and would insist "*el hecho no es un derecho*," – "the fact is not a right." Some cleverly manipulated misperceptions that reform would legitimize appropriation from legitimate property holders, or instantly translate certificates of possession into formal titles. They saw these reforms as threatening the security of the law, ignoring a simple fact: Peru had become a country where the majority were informal owners – which called into question the "security" the law was supposed to provide.

Within the government, there was a small minority very much opposed to the reform but that, for political reasons, claimed to be reformers. This opposition was committed to populist appeasement but not to the kind of deep change the pilot represented. The discrepancy was such that in 1993 we even came across a Peruvian ministry negotiating with an international development bank for funding to "complete" title issuance under the old 1969 Agrarian Reform, and which tried to thwart the pilot by offering to handle the *informales* through the traditional property rights system. Needless to say, these difficulties frustrated us, and meetings with ministry officials to discuss the pros and cons of the old and new system, and respond to their questions, seemed unending.

The opposition also took on an international dimension, spawning a debate among some academics who held to the traditional model of segmentation and those who specialized in land and property. Two camps emerged in the debate both in and outside Peru. The *traditionalists* refused to accept any change in the way things had always been done beyond simple fine-tunings and reorganizations. The *reformers* favored change, realizing that the State needed to do a

---

The Ugly Side of Opposition

The armed revolutionaries, or *guerilleros*, were a particularly ugly side of the opposition, and they could be menacing. One little known fact is that considerable resistance to our reforms came directly from the *Senderistas* and MRTA, who had exploited inept governance and capitalized on the lack of trust and partnership between the government and the citizenry. The radicals offered protection and contract enforcement to all those seeking a "title" or a place in the formal structure of the State – some of them were people living in the new urban settlements or those in rural areas with certificates of possession who lived in constant fear of being dispossessed.

The Ugly Side of Opposition – *continued*

The guerillas did not welcome reforms that would improve governance, including property-rights reforms. Our team experienced this first hand during an "awareness campaign" introducing the new system in an urban community outside of Lima. We planned to present the idea to citizens at the community hall and answer any questions they might have. The visit required approval and an advance clearance from the community leader who arranged it for a time when the guerillas wouldn't be around.

On that particular evening, things did not work as planned. The sound of repetitive gun shots filled the air, turning everybody's blood cold. There was noise and confusion, the sound of barking and howling, followed by dead dogs raining down through the hall's skylight. Soon after that, armed guerillas marched in, with their faces covered, shouting military-like orders and calling for absolute attention. They broke into partisan songs, hymns and promises to the liberation cause. The message was clear, their warning serious: this was their territory, no one should entertain changing their world. Reforms should be taken elsewhere.

---

better job of creating an environment to enable economic growth and make public services respond to a dynamic market.

Every battle the opposition won meant more time lost for the reform. Meanwhile, the citizens who would benefit from the reform remained marginalized and excluded, with no voice or market access. Opponents, perhaps unknowingly, were handing a victory to the revolutionaries who wanted to increase, not reduce, the number of *informales*.

All this opposition had an effect. Opponents did everything in their power to stop the reform. When the pilot ended, I was told that it would not be extended nationwide because it was not part of the World Bank's standard activities and was perceived as a small, peripheral project – albeit a successful one. I also was told that for political reasons, some in the Peruvian government did not want the effort to go on.

The reform's opponents ignored the significant positive impact of the pilot alone.[30] At any given moment, we could face a new pretext from the naysayers: "banks won't lend to uncreditworthy *informales*, even if you give them property rights," or "it is simply illegal to work with these people," or "we shouldn't reward land invasions." Even though some opponents might have been informal real estate owners themselves, they kept on referring to "those" *informales*, viewing them only as those who lived in the new urban areas. Time and again I would make a presentation to decision makers only to be told that the reform model was "too new" or that the World Bank just "doesn't have enough experience with this issue."

Some of the opposition was quite underhanded. We worked with local private investors, made numerous presentations to Congress and special ministerial committees, and sometimes it looked as if there was agreement for a nationwide program. However, much of it was a charade, as opponents would subtly distort recommendations and introduce all sorts of hurdles. When draft legislation was circulated for approval, the fine print included language that effectively eliminated *Registro Predial* or rendered it ineffective. Opponents sought to have it operate under the rules of the old registry, or add new costly requirements for those using it to obtain obligatory clearance from public notaries. Amazingly, one proposed iteration added a provision, ostensibly for "legal protection," requiring written consent of transfer from the "original" owner listed in the traditional registry – no simple task given the systemic confusion and informality that existed. Considering how almost impossible it was to track transactions, it was absurd, almost as bad as asking for written consent from the original property owners of the 1800s, when Peru's republic was created.

Opportunity for real reform of the informal sector kept us going in the face of opposition. We were heartened by the changes we saw underway and how they affected people's lives, which is described in Chapter 5. Trust mended and created partnerships between citizens, the State and the private sector. Peru's property market came to life and loans were being extended, giving citizens who happened to be *informales* a chance to improve their homes, seek better-paying jobs, and find the place they had always wanted in their own country. Peru's divide between the formal and informal was narrowing.

Like former *informales*, our stock was rising. In 1996, the Peruvian Government took on a full-fledged national reform program. One year later, I was delighted to hear the property rights reforms program in Peru being named a "flagship" by a World Bank Director. At the same time it had become a pleasure to visit communities that participated in the reform process. After the fear, the strong opposition, and the occasional sense of defeat we had experienced, it was satisfying to see that the reforms where taken to heart by the citizens themselves.

5
Results through Partnerships

> *We lived in a notoriously unsafe, crime- and drug-
> infested neighborhood. Everything's changed. Now
> people take pride in fresh paint, new carpeting, new
> faucets and tubs. These homes and this neighbor-
> hood are our own.*
>
> – Deborah Thomas, Washington, DC.

Transforming Unreal Estate is a complex undertaking. It is not an academic exercise, but rather involves finding and implementing a practical solution. It requires taking risks. The devil is in the details. It demands both patience and perseverance, and it cannot succeed without commitment and conviction from the right team of partners. Lasting success requires that it be *market-driven*.

At its core, this transformation is about bringing assets to the market – as we saw in Peru, where we created and implemented a new system that unleashed household savings, most of which had been illiquid, frozen in the walls of homes and land of informal owners. What we accomplished helped open the door to *unbound prosperity*.

In Peru, short-term investors, committed long-term investors, ordinary citizens, owners, leaseholders and

101

local and central authorities became partners in reform as trust was reestablished, and eventually succeeded in making Peru's property market attractive both domestically and internationally. In an environment where informality had been widespread, formal ownership expanded and property-based lending increased, as did owners' individual security and overall economic growth. Reform created new opportunities for individuals and businesses. It opened a new future.

Along the way, Reality Check Analysis was a powerful tool that provided us with the information we needed. It allowed us to bring to life what we knew from theory; that institutions, especially property rights, matter a great deal. It provided an opportunity to demonstrate in practice that if property rights were established formally, the market could, indeed, take care of the rest. Success at each stage of the reform propelled our team into the next phase, helped strengthen our efforts and kept us going despite every challenge and difficulty.

Those of us involved in making the institutional reform happen witnessed the gestation of a new market and the transformation of people's lives. It was exhilarating! In the first four years alone, the institutional change in Peru created formal property rights for 4 million people and, after subtracting the US $66 million investment for the reform, netted some US $1.7 billion in property value for Peruvians.[1] Benefits ranged from increased security of ownership to increased investment, to significantly improving the everyday life of children and women. Those benefits were quantified in surveys conducted as the reforms were put in place and the dramatic results are shown in this chapter.

It all became a reality because the reform process brought forward determined leaders from the public and private sector, and from among the citizens, who formed partnerships that deepened the reforms and moved them forward through tipping points. Previously, these types of government officials would have been perceived as "high political risk takers" and those in the private sector as "mavericks." But the emergence of these unusual characters was needed to make the reforms real and help build a stronger property market.

An important tipping point was reached when private financial groups began lending to newly formal property holders. One important private sector partner was Grupo Carsa, which had considerable success offering construction and consumer finance to clients of the new registry in 1994 and 1995. Its manager, Pablo Bustamante, continued to press for further reform after the pilot ended by emphasizing the social and economic benefits of the new property rights system to ministers and members of Congress. Bustamante realized that what was good for his country was also good for his company. Grupo Carsa's business would benefit if Peru increased the number of formal property rights holders, and Bustamante was instrumental in having his firm provide operational funding for the new registry after the pilot ended in 1993. Over the next three years, more than 100,000 new properties were added to the new registry. Grupo Carsa later formed a bank targeting this new market segment and issued securities against its loan portfolio which were then purchased by private commercial banks such as Citibank.

The success of private lenders in Peru was a break from the past. Numerous government interventions had discouraged private investment and Peru's development banks – targeting agriculture, housing, mining, and industry – had pushed out private lending in these sectors, reducing the number of financing options available. Moreover, in the past, the high risk associated with the *insecurity* of property rights meant that if commercial banks made any property-based loans, they typically were limited to highly-regarded citizens who owned sizeable properties in prime urban areas, or owned large farms whose crops could be used as a sort of collateral.

Private lenders began to find Peru's property market attractive as the macroeconomic reforms of the early 1990s provided an environment in which the new property rights system reforms could develop and prosper. Macroeconomic adjustment successfully defeated hyper-inflation, deregulated the banking sector and trade, eliminated development banks and many indirect subsidies for housing finance and construction. Competition among private lenders increased along with transparency, reducing moral hazard and curbing corruption.

The signs of the emergence of a robust property market attracted new champions from Congress and the executive branch. One of our main supporters was Jaime Yoshiyama, then minister of the presidency. Yoshiyama, a former businessman educated at Harvard University, spearheaded the institutional reform effort, bringing the same skillful precision he had shown in the successful privatization program in the early 1990s.[2] Involving government in a partnership for change led to a second important tipping point. In 1996, Peru's government agreed to extend the property rights reforms *nationwide*, with funding from the World Bank. The government created a new commission, Cofopri, which would work in tandem with the new registry, Registro Predial, sharing the process of transforming Peru's property market. The implementation began in 1998 and a political choice was made to start the reform in urban areas, home to more than four million *informales* who owned approximately one million properties.[3] Rural areas remained under the traditional system, with the expectation that they eventually would be brought under the new system, which occurred in 2002.

Was it necessary to establish a new organization to expand the property rights reforms nationwide? In extending reforms to the entire country, we had to juggle two conflicting objectives. One was to develop and maintain the property registration system using the new registry, while at the same time handling the rapid transformation of a very large number of informal properties to formal ones – enough to create the necessary market momentum. Cofopri proved essential in managing the latter. It was structured to facilitate the work of the new registry so that it would not be distracted by non-core business processes at the start of its operation nationwide. Cofopri and the new registry combined their operations and brought the new property rights system to most of Peru's larger cities in less than four years, surpassing the target of one million registrations.

The nationwide reforms marked the end of the beginning. The principles of the reform finally had been fully endorsed and a new period of deeper institutional change started. We monitored changes every day – both social and economic. We introduced a dynamic, flexible and self corrective system for Cofopri and the new registry to adjust to the types of informality that surfaced daily in the transformation process.

It was important to ensure that the information on the properties, or "rights" would be used by the financial sector. To that end, we worked with investors and bankers and created alternative methods to evaluate credit risk associated with new formal property rights holders who had been *informales* and thus had no formal credit standing. At the same time, we worked with government to broaden regulatory changes affecting housing construction, housing finance, valuation and foreclosure. All these actions were designed to bring the private sector on board as a strong partner.

We also viewed those using the new system as partners who could offer valuable feedback about how the reforms were working, with an eye towards any necessary improvements. We wanted to hear from *the new* clients – be they a small property owner, banker or utility company executive. We established internal quality control mechanisms that would set off "red lights" whenever there was a problem at the new registry affecting the speed, cost or quality of the service. This quality control process was very important in ensuring the new system worked smoothly, left clients satisfied and turned them into major advocates of the overall reform effort.

Measuring the impact

Being able to quantify the social and economic benefits was itself an important accomplishment, because before-and-after data mapping the development of institutions rarely are available. Comparisons are difficult because institutions usually take so very long to consolidate and create robust property-based markets – often longer than anyone's lifetime. However, by introducing massive, widespread reforms to Peru's property rights system, which affected so many people in such a short time, we saw noticeable, positive results right from the start. A baseline survey of 2,750 Peruvian urban households was conducted in 2000 – just as the reform was first unfolding and communities were experiencing changes in how they had long operated. The impact of the reform is noteworthy not only in absolute terms but also in comparison to past efforts by the Peruvian authorities.

The data show that people who had received formal property rights felt much more secure as owners. They began to trust that under the new system, the State would enforce their rights of ownership.

Some 94 percent of Peruvians with formal property rights perceived a high level of security in their ownership – double that of those lacking any documentation (see Figure 5.1). Notably, this perceived security also eclipses the level of security felt by those holding "informal" documentation, such as property tax receipts, a certificate of possession or a "title" issued by a mayor or other political official. In an environment of pervasive informality, the issuance of *any* paper with some kind of "official" stamp could give informal owners an increased sense of security. The cohesion and solidarity that comes from living in stable communities where neighbors remain neighbors for a very long time also helps explain

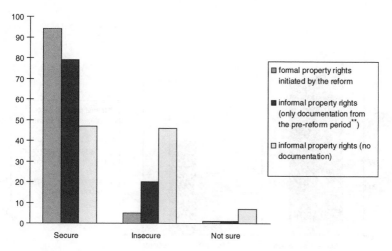

Figure 5.1   Perceptions of security in property rights in Peru*

* in percent of relevant respondents to 2000 household survey
** purchase agreement, municipal, and other "titles" issued prior to the reform discussed herein; the figures represent the average among holders of these types of documentation
Note: There are three categories of property rights formal property rights, as enacted by the reform; informal property rights with some documentation prior to the reform and informal with no documentation.
Source: Apoyo Consultoria (2000), household survey.

why 79 percent of those with informal documentation nevertheless perceived their ownership as secure.

Reforms did more than change perceptions, however. It is the security created by the new property system that generated tangible social and economic benefits for formal property owners that were not available to informal owners, as demonstrated in subsequent figures. It is formal property rights that spurred investment in property, and it is only with formal documentation that we see a marked increase in private-sector loans, for instance.

Not surprisingly, the more secure owners feel, the more they invest in their property. People are more interested in making improvements to their properties when they are indisputably the owners. As Figure 5.2 shows, the

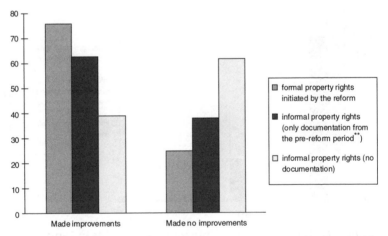

Figure 5.2 Investment in property improvements in Peru with property rights*

* in percent of relevant respondents to 2000 household survey; including construction of walls, repairs to roof and floors, addition of bedrooms
** purchase agreement, municipal, and other "titles" issued prior to the reform discussed herein; the figures represent the average among holders of these types of documentation
Source: Apoyo Consultoria (2000), household survey.

survey found that fully 75 percent of Peruvians with formal property rights used their new tradable asset as a means to invest in and improve their property. Only 39 percent of those with no documentation did the same.

Since the survey was conducted just as the reform was beginning, it was difficult to measure the *actual* increase in property value resulting from formal property rights. Rather, the survey measured perceptions, and we see in Figure 5.3 that *formal* ownership translates into a perception of increased property value, which in turn leads owners to care more about their property and its improvement.

Notably, confidence in the formal property right can be seen from the start in the number of property

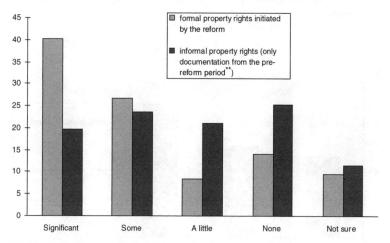

Figure 5.3 Perceptions of increased property values in Peru after obtaining property rights*

* in percent of relevant respondents to 2000 household survey
** purchase agreement, municipal, and other "titles" issued prior to the reform discussed herein; the figures represent the average among holders of these types of documentation
Source: Apoyo Consultoria (2000), household survey.

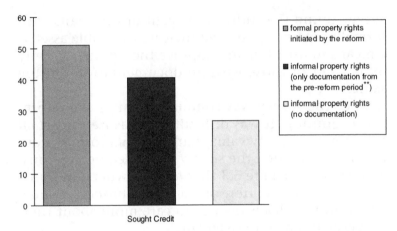

Figure 5.4 Households that solicited loans based on property rights*

* in percent of relevant respondents to 2000 household survey
** purchase agreement, municipal, and other "titles" issued prior to the reform discussed herein; the figures represent the average among holders of these types of documentation
Source: Apoyo Consultoria (2000), household survey.

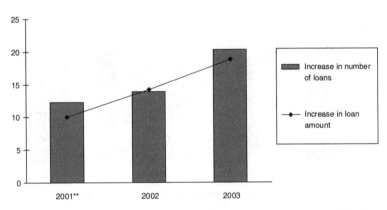

Figure 5.5 Number and amount of loans to property owners after the reform*

* in percent of increase over previous period
** previous period for 2001 is the year 2000
Source: CIP/COFOPRI.

owners soliciting credit (see Figure 5.4). Owners with formal property rights are more likely to seek credit than those with informal property – likely a result of the higher net worth that comes from formal property rights, increasing the expected income stream for property owners and thus signaling lower risk to lenders.

As demand for credit by newly formal owners increased over time, the banking sector expanded the supply and type of credit available, offering more loan products, including more collateral-based loans. As Figure 5.5 shows, the average loan amount increased steadily over time, as has the number of loans issued.

Another benefit that people perceive from turning their homes into *formally* tradable assets is that it frees them from having to be on alert continually for proving their ownership. Appropriate formal institutions, more specifically, appropriate *property rights systems*, have effects on employment by freeing individuals to be more flexible in their choice of work. The *choice* that comes with formal ownership alters the fabric of society, particularly for those seeking to expand their professional skills and enhance their income, since labor mobility leads to potentially higher income and greater opportunities. More Peruvians gained access to the formal labor market; the security that comes with formal property rights reduced the pressure on individuals to work in cottage industries and allowed them to pursue better jobs elsewhere. As fewer Peruvians felt homebound in their employment, the overall number of hours worked outside the home rose by 17 percent and the possibility of working in cottage industries fell by 47 percent. This had an important impact on Peru's women and children, who are primarily responsible for "guarding the property."[4]

Women accounted for more than half of the newly registered formal property owners, in strong contrast to the past when there was a legal bias to register property in the name of the man, who was viewed as the head of the family. Women's wealth and work choices increased as formal property rights expanded. Benefits also spread to children's daily life. After property owners obtained formal property rights, the likelihood that their school-aged children would work decreased by 28 percent. Children were able to spend more time on school activities and the increase in school attendance meant more children had access to school-based preventive health care programs, such as vaccinations.

Peru's small middle class strengthened as people previously locked out of the formal market began to participate in formal economic and financial market activities. The broken *trust* between the individual and State authorities started to show signs of healing. Enforcement of the rule of law became an increasingly important issue of shared legitimacy among homeowners and communities as a whole. For instance, people began to request police presence in their neighborhoods to protect their property and their communities – a marked change from the old mistrust towards the State and reliance on guerrilla groups to fill the void. The new property rights system, coupled with the overall macroeconomic improvements, was eliminating the desire for "alternative governance" among Peruvians. People were returning to their communal activities openly and without fear. These were all signs of the renewal of *social capital*. The theoretical benefits of establishing property rights were now a reality, helping heal social rifts and increase social cohesion.

Transformation sticks when there is trust

Success in both social and economic terms secured the momentum for property rights reform. It did not merely persist but thrived, making formal rights the norm and not the exception it had been in the past. A reversal seems remote. Banks so far have been eager to work with newly formal property owners in Peru. The new property rights system already has endured challenges by three successive national governments. Peruvians trust the system and the institutions in question, which guarantee the irreversibility of the reforms – irrespective of who happens to be the government leader or who administers the relevant organizations. It is not a Fujimori phenomenon or a World Bank phenomenon. Institutions succeed when people use them all the time, without regard for – or even remembering – the name of an individual associated with them.

The central role of trust in the system cannot be overemphasized. Markets and exchange *do not* operate absent trust. Trust reduces uncertainty and allows positive incentives to take effect. People engage in transactions because they have confidence that the system is functional and of benefit to them. Conversely, a system based only on obligation, fear and imposition eliminates incentives, is costly to enforce and undermines the legitimacy of written rules. In fact, such a system often spurs people to violate the rules. Even when contracts are negotiated in a modern, sophisticated economy, it is not the written, legal obligation that motivates compliance, or fear of consequences for non-compliance; it is trust in the system and between the parties that makes the deal possible.

Failed attempts to establish formal real estate in countries where property registration is mandatory illustrate this point, as many of these countries continue to experience informal ownership. Laws that simply *obligate* people to register their properties do not guarantee compliance or eliminate the problems associated with widespread "unreal estate." What was lacking in those countries made the difference in Peru: *reviving trust*. It was the fulcrum of the design.

Property rights reform in Peru was applied with an approach that was completely different from what had been done in the past. It did not view the problem as a series of self-contained issues that could be tackled by respective specialists in sociology, anthropology or history. It did not segment the problem or promote technocratic solutions. It did not rely on computers, traditional cadastral and titling work, sophisticated financial reengineering or on legal and legislative approaches alone. Its objective was nothing less than the development of a robust real estate market.

As trust had been severed in Peru, the reforms focused on repairing it. One problem was that the State was seen as an entity divorced from the real interests of the citizens and the market, not as a partner that would help bring about growth and socioeconomic benefits. Private-sector lenders had to be enticed to a market they had previously avoided, in part because government policies made it unattractive.

The *new* property rights system changed this environment. We placed the property-rights owners and their trust at the center of the new property rights system. We constructed a system that was easy for owners to use, and which provided reliable information for private-sector lenders. We needed to ensure that the new registry system would serve its primary function of information exchange and be a clearinghouse of property rights data, including registration, valuation, and conflict resolution. We sought to reduce distortions in the creation and use of property data by constructing incentives to encourage property owners to provide complete and accurate information, which would foster investment, encourage creditors to lend and developers to build.

Risk and Unreal Estate

Informal market environments are not as risky as they appear to outsiders because they rely on trust, reputation and the eagerness of those in such environments to *be formal*. For example, most informal owners pay property taxes, which they see as an easy way to prove their legal status as property owners. As discussed in Chapter 1, to be informal is a condition of irregularity and a symptom of institutional malaise rather than illegality. Once investors recognize this and are able to evaluate it appropriately, they can invest and do business with the goal of doing well by doing good. Investors will bank on the trust and willingness of players to participate, offering products that create social and economic benefits, signaling the fact that this is a real opportunity. In turn, this attracts more private investment.

Eventually, property owners became more trusting of the new written institutions, and private investors and entrepreneurs came to believe that Peru's once illiquid property market truly was being transformed. Private investors abandoned their traditional reluctance toward this sector of the economy as they began to recognize the *opportunity* of new business and investment prospects. These investors moved toward a long-term investment perspective and formed partnerships with the State to ensure that government would maintain the new system and not reverse course.

Private investors also built partnerships with the newly formal property owners – as new clients. The private sector enjoyed a larger slice of pie in a sector it had once eschewed while the size of the pie itself grew – benefiting all.

It became increasingly clear in Peru that these sorts of reforms can happen only if the participants have a *genuine* stake in the changes. Delegating the task to outside development agencies isn't sufficient and I would go as far as suggest that it is not even appropriate since these agencies have no real claim in the matter.

The emergence of partnerships is in a sense, the litmus test of whether these types of reforms are working. If partnerships develop, it means trust has been rebuilt and that changes are viewed as legitimate. In Peru, property asset values rose, supply and demand for credit increased and investment grew. The elements of property rights reform are not unique to Peru, however, and they may be applied to partnerships and reform efforts elsewhere, including in more sophisticated markets.

What to look for in a partner

Why are partnerships so vital for a reform? Trust implies a sense of partnership among those who share a stake in costs, responsibilities and outcomes. As noted previously, when trust erodes, transactions occur in sub-optimal conditions, with short-term opportunism supplanting long-term, relationship-based exchanges. Trust expresses a credible commitment to a shared goal among those involved in the agreed-upon exchange. The State could be one of the partners only if its laws and regulations truly represent the needs of the constituents and are seen as legitimate. Citizens and investors will view the State as a serious partner only when the State's policies clearly reflect market needs.

A partnership can be initiated by entrepreneurs, the State or the citizens. Those leading the effort need a particular combination of skills and personality. It is imperative that they be creative visionaries who know the pulse of a country's market and are willing to make long-term commitments. They need to be bold, patient and tenacious. They need to subscribe to the view of doing well for themselves while doing good for society, a philosophy summarized as one of adding value by creating value.

Investing with the dual aims of making a profit and helping strengthen society is not a novel idea in the private sector. It is found among investors in more modern and consolidated markets. They are not speculators who jump into a market looking for a fast return and quick exit. These patient, long-term players seek to increase value and asset performance over time.

There are companies and foundations in the world that share this view and so would appear to make a good private-sector partner. Two examples from the US show how a bank and a single woman brought about changes in distressed communities by acting in partnership with others.

Bank of America, one of the largest banks in the United States,[5] has a history of stepping in to rebuild communities' real estate. After the devastating San Francisco earthquake of 1906, founder A.P. Giannini supplied credit to Bay Area residents on the basis of a handshake. Today, Bank of America has a major community development banking business that provides long-term financing in disadvantaged communities. Although it does not get involved in establishing property rights, it focuses on revitalizing neighborhoods using an "inclusive" approach based on the recognition that the people who know what's best for their community are the people who live there.[6]

Bank of America has committed US $750 billion US nationwide to its Community-Development program over ten years. Although US laws encourage banks to lend to underserved areas, Bank of America has developed an aggressive approach loans investments and real estate development to revitalize distressed and underserved neighborhoods. While the program is very different from the traditional commercial banking model, it does share a common denominator: the bank is in this market to make a profit. "We believe that taking capital into *distressed* communities is good business," Bank of America Senior Vice President Brian Tracey explained to me. "When we help these people become first-time homebuyers, we do good in the community and do well for our company. As neighborhood economies become more sustainable, we as a business – and all businesses – prosper."

Bank of America recognizes that low-income borrowers may need services it doesn't offer, including credit counseling, so it identifies and supports organizations that do such work, provide grants through the Bank of America Foundation and enrolling volunteers to help prepare potential homebuyers to become borrowers. Bank of America even has crafted specific mortgage loans for borrowers in these communities that count non-traditional sources of credit history.

Consider this partnership between Bank of America and the Central American Resource Center (CARECEN), a non-profit organization that serves Latino communities in the Columbia Heights, Adams-Morgan, and Mt Pleasant neighborhoods of Washington, DC.

Washington, DC, like many US cities, is filled with run-down and crumbling apartment buildings in slum neighborhoods. Decades of ineffective housing policies have undermined incentives to maintain rental properties. Landlords and tenants alike misuse and abuse these properties. Building codes are routinely violated; absentee owners ignore the deterioration and concentrate on getting rents out of the tenants.

When the city condemned some apartment buildings in Mt Pleasant in 2000, CARACEN and Bank of America worked together with federal housing authorities and the National Council of *La Raza*[7] to help a group of tenants purchase the buildings and convert them into attractive and affordable homes. In addition to US $1.6 million in financing, Bank of America provided technical assistance to educate CARECEN's management about housing finance. The Bank in return received the *possibility* of providing mortgages in the future to CARECEN's clients, and won an important reputation in the neighborhood – based on *trust*.

Consider another example from Anacostia – a segregated, violent, drug-infested, low income part of Washington, DC. There, Bank of America targeted the long-neglected Hillsdale neighborhood for intensive investment as part of its five-year neighborhood revitalization program focusing in four US cities. Since 1995, it has made equity investments of more than US $1.8 million in an apartment complex that was largely boarded up and vacant and provided US $5.8 million for construction and renovation. Later at the request of residents the bank developed affordable town homes and multi-unit apartment in a neighboring block replacing vacant and dilapidated buildings.

By creating value in these communities, Bank of America increases the wealth base of low-income property owners who live in partly informal areas of the United States. As a result, the wealth base becomes more sustainable and profitable for *all* parties involved.

While Bank of America is working with distressed communities, it operates in a country where formal property rights generally exist. When property rights are weak or non-existent and assets are thus not tradable, change cannot rely solely on such private-sector partners. The public sector must also become an active partner for change, and that requires *political will*. However, leaders may also emerge from among the citizenry. We see this in the story of Deborah Thomas, a Washington, DC, native who spent nearly five years fighting for control of apartment buildings on 14th and W Streets, N.W., a once blighted, crime-ridden neighborhood.

In March 2000, DC's city administration began a campaign to force landlords of low-income, multi-unit properties to clean up and maintain their buildings, even arresting a handful of landlords for housing violations. In most cases, the buildings were condemned as unlivable and residents faced eviction, offering another example of the results of failed housing policies: rather than resolve problems, they merely move them elsewhere.

Thomas learned that the city had condemned 1418 14th Street, N.W., the building she was raised in and where her mother still lived. At a press conference a day later, Thomas put the city on the spot and demanded that the mayor not victimize tenants by kicking them out and sending them to live in temporarily in group shelters. Thomas, a high school graduate and former welfare recipient, immediately contacted potential allies on the city council, educated herself on tenants' rights and rallied the residents to take charge of solving the problem themselves. The tenants managed to keep the building open and didn't have to disrupt their daily lives, work or childcare arrangements.

Thomas did not stop there, however. "We needed to secure *our* homes," she explained to me. Over several weeks, Thomas successfully led an effort to engage the mayor's office in negotiations that resulted in a major victory, allowing tenants of the building she grew up in to purchase the entire building from the landlord for a nominal US $1 payment. Tenants who would have been left homeless became owners, and each received US $114,000 when they chose to sell the building to a developer in August 2003.

After this successful experience, Thomas had learned the ins and outs of regulations, and how the city, developers and private lenders worked. She used this knowledge to go one step further in her new home, in a complex of three rundown apartment buildings on the same block of W Street. Thomas organized fellow tenants and sought financing that would allow them *to purchase* the property outright and renovate it.

The tenants bought the buildings with US $3.4 million in loans from the DC government, the National Cooperative Bank and a church foundation's housing assistance program. Another US $8.6 million of bank loans covered the cost of repairing the aging property. Today, residents are owners of a newly-renovated apartment complex. Pride is back on this block as the new homeowners care for their building and work to make the block cleaner and drug free.

Thomas explained it simply at one public meeting to debate the matter, saying: "We have a lifetime of investment on this block."[8]

What Deborah Thomas did in Washington, DC demonstrates what Brian Tracey of Bank of America noted – that residents know what is best for their communities. Given the appropriate information and an environment where that information could be used, the tenants association showed that residents could make the best of a market. Secure in their property rights, they sought to improve what they genuinely own. In a slum where there had been no incentives for the previous owner or renters to do anything but let the property rot, these residents used the tradable asset – ownership of their building – to secure financing for improvements. Thomas had figured out how to bring together government, private-sector financing institutions and citizens, and make things work for the benefit of all partners.

For property rights reform, the *commitment* of a high-level government official is crucial. A State agency, and preferably a committed *State leader*, has to be ready and willing to undertake all necessary changes, including legal and regulatory reforms, to benefit constituents.

The politician therefore needs to operate beyond short-term populist political gains and consciously strive for policy changes that will bring about positive social and economic outcomes. Often, the public must push politicians and other government officials to embrace reform and assume the mantle of leadership. Reform must appeal to the politician's altruism – to do something good for the "common" people – and balance that against the interest in benefiting the elite, who may not be personally affected by informality and thus may not believe reform is necessary. Often, opposition forces hide behind the elite.

Just as investors may have a short-term horizon, the lack of a *long-term* vision poses a problem in the public sector, where many politicians have a short-term view dictated by election cycles. Any politician who agrees to work for institutional reform will need to overcome some major obstacles, from open political opposition to subtle political pressure. Politicians can mute opposition or render it irrelevant if they can clearly articulate the societal benefits of the reform. Communicating and persuading the public about these benefits will be crucial in such efforts.

For the State, the reform offers particular benefits. A well-functioning property rights system makes the overall work of the State clearer, more predictable and more accountable. It lowers transaction costs. It rebuilds trust. It legitimizes the very work and existence of the public sector, not through handouts and entitlements but by involving people in markets at the level of their properties – land and homes – which represent their honor and their sense of belonging to a community.

A reform that creates formal property rights establishes new market opportunities, and hence new profit opportunities, across the board. It helps promote the use of financial assets by the rich *and* the poor. It creates greater economic security. While it allows for a more even distribution of wealth, it does so not by expropriation but by increasing the size of the "pie" and increasing wealth, along with social homogeneity. In short, for all concerned, the reform creates a win-win situation.

Arguments to the public sector generally, and politicians in particular, regarding these benefits must appeal to the best notions of empowerment – both for the politicians and for constituents. Thus *democracy* plays a central role in the reform argument. Here we are talking about the notion of economic voice and choice, not simply casting a vote in an election. Formal property rights create choice for people and the means by which they can better themselves and their communities. When the public sector embraces reforms that create this choice, it builds wealth for citizens. More broadly, an environment with formal, legitimate institutions is a more stable environment, with greater social cohesion and less social discontent. These reforms build social homogeneity and wealth, ensuring support for the system over the long term.

How do we engage the private sector? The State? Who leads? There are no easy answers. Sometimes, circumstances – and crises – create the conditions for leaders to emerge. Timing and environment, for instance, are critical factors – as we shall see in Chapter 6.

6
Solving the Puzzle

> *Strategy without tactics is the slowest route to victory. Tactics without strategy is the noise before defeat.*
> – Sun Tzu (BC 535–228) – Chinese military strategist

"Unreal estate" and dysfunctional institutions are no local phenomena. They exist across continents and throughout the developed and developing world. We have made the case that they are not specific to any one nationality or culture but reflect informality and result from inappropriate institutions, policies, and poor or missing incentives.

Institutional reform is the solution to the "unreal estate" trap, but only if done correctly. In Peru, we were able to succeed because we correctly diagnosed the problem as inappropriately modeled institutions, not organizational lag, and knew what needed to be done to correct it because of using Reality Check Analysis. This methodology allowed us to uncover the most relevant aspects of history that had affected the formal rules then in place, as well as people's behavior and incentives. It helped us understand the way institutions and organizations developed over time and determine if their problems were chronic or recent, deep or superficial. It helped us identify partners to work with us along the way – those who would have a stake in the outcome and thus, a strong interest in the changes. What became clear from our work was that institutional reforms need to be holistic to succeed.

A holistic solution to the jigsaw puzzle

Employing this new analytical tool resulted in a *cross-sector* approach to designing a property-rights reform geared to local conditions. In Peru, this meant a head-on confrontation with traditional ways of thinking regarding investment and economic development interventions. We broke through the tradition of segmentation; that is focusing on a specific technical area, such as law or engineering, or on a particular facet of the economy, such as agriculture or industry. We broke through the reliance on technocratic specialists working in isolation from one another. We sought to connect the public and private sectors and promote their working together in profitable partnership; something that had not been done effectively in the past. We also broke with the habit of addressing organizations and ignoring institutions because what they comprise – laws, rules, regulations and history – are considered too sensitive or too political, or simply too complicated to tackle. We favored an approach that encompassed *all* of these areas and cut across all the relevant sectors.

Institutions are what hold together a complex, multidimensional socioeconomic puzzle. Ignoring them, misunderstanding them or focusing on one to the exclusion of others makes it nearly impossible to implement a successful reform. As noted earlier in this book, informal markets persist due to an intractable institutional structure – institutions and organizations that do not meet the needs of society – coupled with negative incentives for all those using them and affected by them, including investors, lenders, the State and ordinary citizens.

We needed to introduce a different relationship among investors, policymakers, economists and technocrats without eliminating or reducing the richness of their analysis and rigor. It was common in the 1990s to hear economists and technocrats at the World Bank or similar agencies discuss policy design in the context of a "perfect world" scenario. Such scenarios were based on numerous assumptions intended to make exchange fully predictable. In a way, this reflected an acceptance of segmented policies and interventions and the assumption that in the end, the separate pieces would all fit together nicely like a jigsaw puzzle. The world, though, is far from perfect. It is full of ideas and realities that do not always fit together. In real life, multiple market sectors rarely fit perfectly. They are dynamic and affected by exogenous factors. The mismatches create wrinkles that often lead to informality, and unfortunately, these very wrinkles are what bother many specialists, including economists and technical "experts."

Using our new analytical methodology, we learned not only that the pieces do not always fit together, but also that sometimes the pieces or even the overall picture will change shape over time. This is precisely why reforms that affect only organizations and create "model" structures and procedures, or reforms that address technical issues alone cannot work. Furthermore, it would be dangerous to preempt and eliminate all institutional problems, such as levels of informality, with one blanket initial reform. It is risky to assume at the beginning of an institutional reform effort that every level of institutional mismatch that could lead to informality – and in the case of property, "unreal estate" – can be and has been accounted for in advance. In the real world, layers of informality are stripped away only after the reform has begun. Such approaches move the pieces around, may increase stress on the system and make it even harder to *solve* the puzzle.

A holistic approach takes the broadest view of the problem. It addresses the creation and usage of the asset information represented in the "right" – the upstream and downstream applications of property rights – to produce a tradable asset. It allows reformers to understand how to design reforms that will restore trust among market participants, thus creating the *impetus* for a more dynamic real estate market. In Peru, Reality Check Analysis helped identify what various participants needed and expected so that the upstream and downstream elements of the reform would be designed appropriately. Our holistic approach meant we were not content to address the existing segmented environment by getting specialists, policymakers and others to exchange notes and work together; this would not create a sufficiently strong bond between the various segments. Rather, we focused on the links between all segments to reach the desired objective. We created incentives for the specialists to *merge* their individual skills, analytical rigor and knowledge in support of a single, overriding goal: to create a *whole* solution based on enduring principles of property rights.

Unbound prosperity, however, demands a *strategy* that is tailored to the local realities of the country and its market. This strategy must be based on a set of *principles* that remain constant in any effort to transform "unreal estate", see Figure 6.1:

Peru offers an example of a successful property rights reform, providing readers of this book with a road map. Naturally, reformers elsewhere will have to adapt their

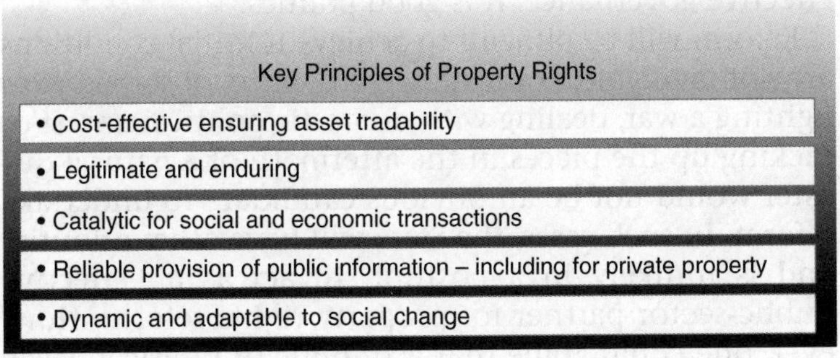

Figure 6.1   Key principles of property rights

strategies to the specific local situation and address questions such as: Is it possible to apply the kind of reform discussed in this book at any time? Or, must there be a *particular* window of opportunity? Are there different perspectives on these questions for the investor, policymaker, and citizen? We will offer some general guidelines in this chapter.

The *when* and *how* of strategy

Timing is all important. Spotting the right window of opportunity to apply the reform is essential. There needs to be a critical mass of political support behind the effort, which starts with a willingness to address the problem, accept the diagnosis and follow through on recommendations. Political will is not necessarily a function of the number of people involved; it can be embodied in one person, such as the head of state, or in a group, such as members of Parliament or executive-branch officials. Political leadership creates a push from the top and gives needed support for reforms that can allow the market to operate efficiently while delivering basic social benefits. In effect, this signals the State's intention to fulfill its promise to citizens to provide effective governance. It is good politics.

Reform will be difficult to achieve if initial conditions are not favorable. For instance, a country absorbed with fighting a war, dealing with domestic political unrest or picking up the pieces in the aftermath of a natural disaster would not be an obvious candidate to undertake reform. In such cases, the State will have other priorities and is unlikely in a position to act as an effective public-sector partner for property rights reform. However, one could argue that economic or political decay may be a very good environment to start the reform, since stress conditions create a common interest for change among most players. This is the interest that can co-opt even latent opposition. In Peru, the institutional reform effort targeting property rights was an effective tool in the fight *against* domestic unrest, proving that reform can succeed even in the most challenging conditions if there is a willingness to give it a chance.

Ideally, institutional reform should unfold hand-in-hand with macroeconomic stability and an overall trend towards open market policies because this is the time when an economy has the greatest need for secure, formal property rights. Timing property rights reform to begin when macroeconomic reform is already underway makes it easier for visionary leaders to emerge from the public or private sector. It provides incentives for private sector participation, strengthens the momentum for the reform and it makes easier to counter opposition. In cases where property rights reforms are not coordinated with macroeconomic reforms, Reality Check Analysis can be a useful tool, but only to identify the challenges, bottlenecks and blind spots that need to be addressed. Reformers must accept that in such a scenario, it may take longer for the reform process to progress.

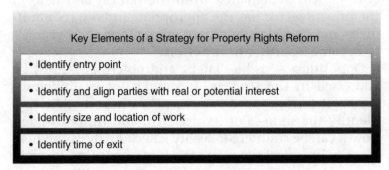

Key Elements of a Strategy for Property Rights Reform

- Identify entry point
- Identify and align parties with real or potential interest
- Identify size and location of work
- Identify time of exit

Figure 6.2   Key elements of a strategy for property rights reform

Certain macroeconomic conditions and financial reforms must be in effect by the time a new property rights system is launched so that it begins under promising conditions. Inflation must be tamed, currency must be stable and private-sector investment and finance must not be crowded out by government policies that create unfair competition and market distortions. If capital markets are barely developed and a country's fundamental macroeconomic conditions are poor, its property market will not become vibrant, even after property rights reform.

The entry point for institutional reform therefore is critical. It is important to be able to identify when and where to begin. While a strategy for nationwide change is ideal, reform can certainly start small. What matters most is that the start springs from a good strategy based on the diagnosis and information provided by Reality Check Analysis. A successful strategy will explore market size and demographics, geography, owners' income levels, community homogeneity and growth potential.

Another key element to a successful strategy involves identifying and aligning constituencies. Reformers must determine who in the State should be engaged, which citizens will benefit first from the reform and who in the private sector has the appropriate interest, commitment and stamina – and particularly long-term vision – to become a partner in the effort.

Opposition – visible, latent and potential – must be addressed in the strategy. It should not be underestimated. Reformers need to determine where it originates, identify the sources of its strength, and think through how it can be countered. Reality Check Analysis can help identify historical types and levels of opposition to avoid repeating past mistakes or having to "reinvent the wheel" in learning how to defeat it. A holistic approach would not necessarily confront all opposition up front; instead, it would outline a sequence of actions that would specify when and how to do so.

Finally, a successful strategy must define the *exit* point in cases where the formal property rights principles no longer guide the reform. The State, its private-sector partners, or both, may abandon these principles under certain circumstances; a reform effort cannot be sustained under such conditions. New partnerships may be necessary in such cases. But, even if there are different partners along the way, there must be continuity in the institutional change, regardless of whether it is pushed from the top or from the bottom.

As long as the strategy encompasses these elements, reformers can develop the tactics – tailored to local and national particularities – that will drive the change from inception to successful completion.

How much of a "stomach" does the reformer need to have?

Of course, there will be setbacks. Not all partners will come on board at the same time and the reform process should accommodate this fact. There is also bound to be some second-guessing among the partners about the approach and method of managing the reforms. There may be challenges to the underlying principles. Sometimes, it will seem as if one partner or another is going to force the reform to veer off the holistic path and retreat to the old, comfortable one of segmentation, limiting thinking to a particular *technical* realm of expertise.

Regardless of the size and scope of the reform being undertaken, those leading the reform effort, whether they come from the citizenry, government or the private sector, must be prepared to handle opposition and setbacks. Reforming the institutional basis of a country is a serious undertaking and those who attempt it should anticipate political battles from vested interests, visible and latent, who will strike at the very core of the government's machinery – the public sector bureaucracy– in an effort to staunch reforms. Reformers who have uncovered the underlying reasons for this opposition and who understand the country's history and culture, including how its social contract developed, will be better armed to fight these battles and even succeed in co-opting the opposition.

The principles of formal property rights serve as guideposts for a strategy based on what is uncovered through Reality Check Analysis. The strategy can vary to suit the reality of markets with different characteristics, locations or economic conditions, for instance, so long as the principles of formal property rights are at the foundation.

The design

In most cases, reform efforts will require changes in written rules. There must be an appropriate legal and operational structure for reform to succeed. Rule changes, especially changes to laws, must be broad enough to embrace the principle of property rights fully *without* being overly specific, which allows for multiple interpretations, leading to additional regulation and growing transactions costs. In Peru, three broad, simple laws established the guiding principles of the new property rights system. They brought institutions in line with real life by rescinding the Agrarian Reform Law, acknowledging the right to individual, private, public and communal property, and permitting private real estate transactions and exchanges. *Appropriate institutions* were established to apply the new formal structure that now reflected the new social demand. That made it possible to eliminate numerous agencies and functions involved in defining property rights, each of which had its own special legal and administrative procedures. The outcome was that transaction costs were cut dramatically.

A pivotal change is the *consolidation* of the property rights system, ideally in one entity. The entity can be run as a public or private operation, but in either case its management must be efficient and selected based on merit. Its information must be publicly available and its processes must be transparent. In essence, this is about building or transforming an organization on a market basis. In the case of Peru, success was reflected not only in reduced transactions costs, but also in the rising satisfaction with the registry's service as the registry itself became accountable to clients as well as the State. Clients of the registry have a reasonable expectation of what they need to do to register their property or obtain other services, how long it will take and how much it will cost. They are expected to provide feedback about their experience. Bad service is reprehended – it suggests internal inefficiency or introductions of new regulations. This feedback process allows the system to be *self-correcting* and ultimately better managed. It is impressive to see these changes in Peru.

Checkpoints should be established during the reform process to afford reformers the opportunity to evaluate the effort and make changes along the way if necessary. Building in the ability to adapt the reform and strategy as new levels of informality are uncovered is particularly important. As we have noted, hidden layers of informality cannot be anticipated or known fully at the outset, and the strategy must allow for adjustments based on what is discovered as the process unfolds. In the case of Peru, as the reform proceeded, hundreds of smaller legal, administrative and regulatory changes were made to fix such problems as they came to light.

The high price of ignoring institutions

Property rights serve as the foundation for market development and for effective, long-term economic growth. The principles of formal property rights articulated earlier cannot be ignored. Countries undertaking market reforms that do not address institutions and property rights may score some successes, but in the long run, those reforms will be precarious, not sustainable. Russia and Albania provide two notable examples.

After the fall of the Berlin Wall, marking the end of the Cold War, the Russian Federation emerged from the ashes of the collapsed Soviet Union. Russia turned to the West in the hope for finding a way to prosperity. In 1991, Russia began a massive economic transformation. Privatizations were deemed to be the way to go, shifting production to the private sector on a massive scale and freeing prices from State control. But the new Russia inherited a challenging legacy from the Soviet Union, including ineffective public services, weak public organizations, contracts and compliance obligated by force, and inadequate fiscal discipline. Underneath all of this was a *skepticism* and distrust by citizens in the nation's organizations and bureaucracies.

Efforts to fix the situation through aid and assistance programs increased cynicism and suspicion. In the 1990s, extensive international intervention to help Russia make the transition from a centrally planned economy took the usual segmented approach that overlooked the underlying need to establish formal and legitimate institutions. Market deregulation – including privatization – was undertaken with very weak institutions that could not support change. Without appropriate incentives in place, the entire process was prone to corruption. Deregulation without proper institutional controls and governance benefited a few oligarchs – small private groups that reaped extraordinary profits by controlling markets and having access to government information before others. While oligarchs grew rich thanks to information asymmetry, the newly decentralized Russian administration could not effectively manage the country or operate the few existing institutions and organizations.

By the end of the 1990s, Russians came to view the West quite critically; after all, it had been Western organizations that advocated these changes. The then newly applied policies of decentralization were far from effective; in fact they had created further uncertainty and confusion. The country experienced a sharp rise in poverty – depending on the exact definition of poverty, about 35 percent of the population fell below the poverty line[1] – and escalating rent-seeking behavior.[2] Average Russians grew nostalgic for the old Kremlin with its traditional vertical power, and a general element of equal treatment, and they increasingly came to view the Soviet-era authoritarianism as a better way, possibly even as the only way to get things done.

The situation was exacerbated by Russia's 1998 economic crisis.[3] Its currency had come under pressure and monetary tightening sent short-term interest rates skyrocketing. The subsequent decline in Russian government securities made foreign creditors demand additional collateral, a demand few Russian borrowers could satisfy at a time when the central bank was draining liquidity to defend the exchange rate. Panic grew as international lenders feared insolvencies in the country's financial sector. Indicators such as the annual inflation rate increased from 14.8 percent in 1997 to 85.7 percent in 1999, while the percentage change in GDP reached a negative number in 1998.[4] At this point, the disaster was inevitable.

Russia's difficulties show that when institutions are malfunctioning and trust in a market and society is weak, conditions in a country can erode rather quickly. Sometimes, the distortions can be downright scandalous. The emergence of the pyramid schemes in Albania is another illustration of this phenomenon.

Like Russia, Albania was one of many repressed markets in the Eastern bloc that turned to the West for assistance after the end of the Cold War. Beginning in 1989, Albania took in all types of advice from development agencies and private investors, and by the mid-1990s, the country was a "star performer."[5] Not only were Albania's macroeconomic indicators impressive, but it had quickly absorbed former government employees into private-sector employment, which accounted for more than 75 percent of the domestic workforce by 1996, up from almost nothing just six years earlier. Sali Berisha, Albania's president at the time, was viewed by the West as a man who would pull the country out of its earlier despair and make it a winner.

Unfortunately, something radically different happened – and it seems as if no one saw it coming. It didn't matter that officials from all the multilateral agencies and international advisory bodies were hard at work in the country; the West seemed powerless to prevent the bizarre financial crisis that unfolded – one that took the Albanian economy into a nosedive.

Starting around 1995, *pyramid schemes* – 17 to be exact – sprang up in Albania, orchestrated by a handful of deposit-taking companies. A pyramid scheme is a hierarchical swindling operation that relies on new participants "investing" money which flows into the pockets of those above them in the pyramid. Participants in pyramid schemes typically are lured by promises of very high returns on money they "invest." In the early going, a small number of the earliest investors do receive high payouts, which do not come from any genuine investment but from the inflow of cash from new recruits lower in the pyramid. The liabilities of every such pyramid very quickly exceed the assets, because it generates no income except by attracting new participants. Pyramid schemes eventually collapse for a very simple reason: they rely on an *infinite* number of people to join the pyramid.

The liabilities of the pyramid scheme in Albania – which recruited a staggering *two-thirds* of the country's population – had a nominal value that equaled half of the country's entire gross domestic product![6] Albanians, perhaps heady with the hope of rapidly transforming their quality of life to that of Western Europeans, rushed to sell whatever they could to invest, including their livestock and even their homes.

The Albanian pyramid-schemes crashed completely by early 1997. The country's gross national product growth in 1997 fell by more than 10 percent, when in 1996 it had grown by 9 percent.[7] People who had lost everything poured into the streets of cities and towns throughout the country. Emigration was unbridled.[8]

Albanians who stayed behind formed militias to protect what they had left and to find and punish those they held responsible. Some 2,000 Albanians lost their lives in this period, the victims of street fighting and government attacks.[9]

Some may attribute the emergence of the Albanian pyramid schemes to the "backwardness" of a people who had lived for decades under the yoke of an oppressive regime in a completely controlled economy. But that argument is too easy, and misses much of the real story and true causes of the breakdown. How could this happen to Albania?

Albania was susceptible to pyramid schemes because the country had very fragile institutional structures, which translated into very weak rights and a "confused" social contract. The country opened to a new market setting with *no* understanding of how to create the formal institutions necessary to live in that new world and to reflect Albanian society's needs.

Albania is a telling example of a country where social capital had become very thin. Over the course of its economic and political history, any incentives for people and government to enter into partnerships had faded. Trust among the citizenry in formal institutional structures had become virtually non-existent. Top-down authoritarian rule existed for a long time with little interruption, dating back before the Ottoman Empire in the fifteenth century and continuing in the modern era during the Cold War, under the dictatorship of Enver Hoxha. Albania's society is often characterized as *atomistic*, meaning individuals act and behave based on what benefits them, not their community or society. In fact, matters became even worse during the Hoxha years, when rewarding loyalty to the communist Party and State authority encouraged lying and treachery, even against family members. Trust was severed at the most personal level. This history left Albanians under-standably skeptical of formal institutions, to which they ascribe little legitimacy. Against this backdrop, the pyramid scheme had widespread appeal. Opportunism prevailed and led Albanian society to accept – quite readily – the "one-shot" deals that make up pyramid scheme transactions.

Of course, when the pyramid schemes crashed, it created even more turmoil and erosion of trust in the new State, its perspectives and its formal rules. The pyramid schemes were not the only thing that col-lapsed; Albania's government and its system of law and order also toppled.

Could the Albanian debacle have been avoided? Of course, it is easy to speculate after the fact. Several things are clear, though. Reform in Albania suffered for all the reasons outlined in this book. *Institutional* change was not addressed. Policy reforms had not con-sidered the way in which institutions linked with the social contract of the country. Rebuilding *trust* was not at the center of reforms; instead, the focus was on the usual segmented, technical modifications. Unfortun-ately, such errors and missed opportunities are not limited to Albania, as similar mistakes are evident in other countries that have sought to make the transi-tion from planned to market-based economies.

If we can learn anything from what happened in Albania and Russia, it is that reformers must identify the type of market in which they are working. They must understand social behavior. They must have a firm grasp of all the incentives that have existed historically, because these are what lead citizens to act – or not.

It is worth considering what would have happened in Albania had the State, working in partnership with citi-zens and the private sector, introduced comprehensive reforms, including reforms that established property rights, and created a system that would benefit all. Such a system might have enabled Albanians to profit from the real value of their properties rather than chasing the promise of phantom returns from sham "investments."

Institutional reforms, especially property rights reforms, can succeed provided *willing* partners in the effort – citizens, the private sector and the State – adhere to the underlying principles and move carefully, recognizing that these changes touch the very core of the social contract and the *trust* citizens have in one another, the State and the private sector.

Property rights reform is, after all, all about what people hold dear – their savings, shelter, honor, sense of belonging, sometimes even their identity. Our experience in Peru showed us it was tough to persuade citizens to give information on their most important asset – their land and property. People will offer information about their property in response to a specific reform only when they are convinced that the information will be used appropriately and in a way that benefits them. Otherwise, they will feel manipulated, cheated – even betrayed – which can destroy the possibility of partnership with the State for a long time. Citizens have long-lasting memories of failed reforms that touched them, and future efforts will be hindered if individuals lack faith in the changes or in the State's ability to make *any* changes for the better.

Similarly, the private sector cannot afford the luxury of working with a State that promises but does not deliver. This wastes time and money. Even the private-sector partner who is willing to adopt a long-term vision has to make a profit, and counts on serious partners who understand the private-sector's need for results. A history of failed partnerships, even in decades past, will not be forgotten when the State promises that things will be different "this time." The private sector needs to be convinced that the reform is real; a good design based on the principle of formal property rights will help make the case, but a commitment, including a political commitment to sticking with the strategy, is essential.

Yet private sector participation is crucial. The task of institutional reforms, especially in the area of property rights, is too far-reaching to be left as the sole responsibility of government policymakers and development agencies. It is the business of all, especially investors and everyday citizens.

This book presents a methodology and a practical solution to informal property. Putting it into practice frees people's savings and gives them more choices, including about where and how they work. It is a flexible solution that can be tailored to any market, in developed or developing countries, where malfunctioning institutions distress property values.

This methodology entails making a correct diagnosis of problems, then treating them with a holistic approach. Successful institutional reforms will have broader economic effects; many well-intentioned macroeconomic reforms have foundered because in the long run, they are held together by institutions. Successful institutional reforms will last and yield positive results, seen not only in economic and financial indicators but in the everyday lives of people.

In Peru, this practical solution gave La Reina de la Papa a brighter future as an entrepreneur. In Greece, it could give Ismini some peace of mind, unleash the market value of her property and finally afford her the freedom to dispose of it in the way that she determines best to serve *her* interest. In the United States, it can create more champions like Deborah Thomas who help turn lives around, promote change and improve their neighborhoods. It was this practical solution that created new opportunities and incentives, *attracting* private investment by those who seek long-term gains rather than short-term speculation, which transforms "unreal estate" to real estate.

The problem of "unreal estate" is global, but its solution *local*, and it can lead to unbound prosperity. The approach worked in Peru and it can be repeated elsewhere. Done right, institutional reform of property rights can reduce risk, ambiguity, costs of transactions and create new possibilities for those who hold assets informally by turning them liquid. In such cases, immovable property that once had little formal exchange value is transformed to a marketable asset. What seemed "unreal" becomes real.

Acknowledgments

This book comes out of my experiences as an economics policy-maker and as a private entrepreneur. In both fields I have been faced with the frustrating problem of informality and especially informal property. Investors are reluctant to invest in these areas because they view them as being too risky; for policymakers, the solutions are few and success stories limited.

My work sprang not only from economic theory but also from its application in various efforts to transform informal markets to formal ones. In creating the Reality Check Analysis it was not economic theory that intrigued me but the way people – rich or poor, educated or not – understand how formal markets work and what restricts them. Defining theories of informality is one thing; implementing a successful transformation is something entirely different.

As you have read in these pages, opposition was a major obstacle to such a transformation, and I would be dishonest if I did not admit that I often thought of throwing in the towel. I am, therefore, very grateful to all the people who helped keep me inspired. Some were pivotal in pushing for transformation in Peru; others advocated the idea of formal property in general; and still others were instrumental in helping me write this book.

I would first like to extend my profound gratitude to my family and especially to my parents Yiannis and Elli, who taught me to be resilient. Their generosity and support was a great motivation, especially when times were hardest. I also received support throughout from two other family members who sadly, passed away just before this work was published.

This book would not have been possible without my dedicated reviewers. I must extend my deep thanks for the long hours and effort they put into what sometimes must have felt like an almost endless process. My friend and colleague Alejandro Garro, a legal reform advisor and law professor at Colombia University, contributed most of the legal analysis in Chapter 2, and made a thorough review of the entire manuscript. Subir Lall from the International Monetary Fund, Deputy Division Chief of the World Economics Studies Division, read the chapters again and again, providing inputs and inspiring conversations and debates, for which I am grateful. For his tireless commitment to making the text clear and accurate, I must thank Denis Drechsler, Economist at the Organization for Economic Cooperation and Development (OECD). Gary Reid senior economist and advisor at the World Bank, and Tim Campbell Chairman of the Urban Age Institute, who reviewed my writings with a critical eye, must also be singled out for thanks.

Special thanks go to Jaime Yoshiyama, a great champion of Peru's reforms who, as a reviewer, gave these pages their own reality check. Thanks also to Fernando Cantuarias, my long-time Peruvian colleague and friend who was the legal advisor to the Peruvian reforms and later became head of the agency implementing the reform program; his critique of the book greatly influenced its final shape. Carl Muñana, a senior investment banker who also worked tenaciously on financial reforms in the Peru effort deserves my gratitude for his patience in reviewing the manuscript, as does John McLaughlin, President of the University of New Brunswick and professor of surveying engineering and institutional economist, who reviewed the book with special attention to the technical aspects and history of property and land markets. I also received input and technical reviews from John McKenna, a former World Bank colleague who has followed the technical developments of property since the 1970s. Arthur Domike's comments and timely reviews were invaluable; he provided me with data about the way property and land markets were treated in international politics and economics after 1945 until the 1990s. Both John and Arthur gave a different touch to my research with their inputs on Japan's land reform right after the Second World War. I also must thank Riordan Roett, an influential American political scientist professor at Johns Hopkins University School of Advance International Studies (SAIS). He directed me to important sources and provided me with vital economic and political analysis of the different treatments land and property markets had in Latin America as opposed to post-1945 Japan. I should also thank Pedro Belli a friend and colleague who participated in the original socio-economic cost benefit analysis of the Peru reforms as well as, Alfred Thieme, a friend and fellow economist who reviewed the latest socioeconomic. A special thanks must be also extended to Deborah Thomas for her tireless cooperation during long interviews about her Washington DC informal property stories.

I also wish to thank Brian Tracey from Bank of America for providing information about the bank's programs, and others who supplied information for this book including Roberto Abusada, Carlos Blanco, Pablo Bustamante, Anthony Pell, Adrian Revilla, and Angela Vassiliou.

I wish to extend my warmest thanks to those people who stood by me throughout all the stages of this process and supported me with their generosity and warmth. Raymond Fay read each chapter over and over and listened to my comments and occasional attempts to quit. Nick Panandreou lent his support and experience as an author, Susan Hoskins stood by me when the going was tough, Ricardo Galbis, and Konstantine Antoniades for their generosity.

I would also like to extend very warm thanks to those I worked with in Peru, namely former Economy and

Finance Minister Carlos Boloña, former World Bank Vice President Armeane Choksi, Ricardo Lago, former Chief Economist at the European Bank of Reconstruction and Development and former head of the Peru macroeconomics division at the Inter-American Development Bank. At the World Bank: Demetris Papageorgiou, Geoffrey Shepherd. At the Institute of Liberty and Democracy: Hernando de Soto, Mariano Cornejo, Manuel Mayorga, Maria del Carmen Delgado, Luis Aliaga and Edgardo Mosqueira.

Special thanks to James McCall, a good friend since my graduate school years who inspired the title of the book. For the laborious task of editing this book, I must thank Scott Cooper. I should also thank Judy Burns, for her final editing review and my friend and colleague Vivien Altman.

I must also present my gratitude to all those whose stories I present in this book, some of whom are faceless and nameless, others are: La Reina de la Papa, Rita, José and Ismini.

For the production of this book, I wish to extend my gratitude to INSEAD, where I am a Visiting Scholar, with special thanks to Gordon Redding, Director of the Euro-Asia and Comparative Research Center, and to Charlotte Butler Research Studies Manager at INSEAD who supported me along the way.

There are many others I have met who have provided me support, advice, guidance or simply stimulating discussion. Although I do not mention them all by name, I do extend my warmest gratitude and ask them to forgive me for not naming them individually.

As the author of this book I take responsibility for any mistakes you may find in these pages and would like to put it on record that I have not received payment for any data included that relates to Bank of America or COFOPRI or another organization.

Notes

Chapter 1 Informality and Unreality

1 *Institutional Economics* and *New Institutional Economics* define transactions costs as "the costs of resources utilized for the creation, maintenance, use and change of institutions and organizations" (Erik G. Furubotn and Rudolf Richter (1997), *Institutions and Economic Theory – The Contribution of the New Institutional Economics*, Ann Arbor: University of Michigan Press, p. 40). Transactions costs include the costs of defining and measuring claims as well as utilizing and enforcing rights.

2 Hernando de Soto (2000) *The Mystery of Capital: Why Capitalism Triumphs in the West and Fails Everywhere Else*, New York: Basic Books, p. 35.

3 George Akerloff (1970) *The Market for Lemons – Quality Uncertainty and the Market Mechanism*, in *Quarterly Journal of Economics*, pp. 488–500.

4 Joe Wallis and Brian Dollery (1990) *Market Failure, Government Failure, Leadership and Public Policy*, New York: St. Martin's Press.

5 Mercantilist economies are characterized by high regulation, strong bureaucratic control, and a limited number of market players. See, for example, Eli F. Heckscher (1955) *Mercantilism*, London: George Allen and Unwin, revised second edition, ed. by Ernst F. Söderlund. (Originally published as *Merkantilisment: Ett led i den ekonomiska politikens historia*, Stockholm: P.A. Norstedt and Söner, 1931).

6 Some countries even now suffer from the existence of this kind of closed elite that controls resources and keeps primary markets from developing and becoming more robust. For instance, in the Philippines, a small elite runs the banking system and exercises its control irrespective of the government in power. See Paul D. Hutchcroft (1998) *Booty Capitalism – The Politics of Banking in the Philippines*, Cornell University Press.

7 Heckscher (1955).

8 Ibid.

9 Ibid.

10 A "social contract" regulates a person's moral and/or political obligations toward society, which – in exchange – opens the

possibility of a disciplined and well-organized communal life according to the rules and regulations set forth by the very members of society. Although Greek philosophers of the antiquity (e.g. Socrates) already considered the necessity of an implicit agreement between individuals and the society to regulate communal life, the concept of a "social contract" was born by modern political theory. Important works include Thomas Hobbes' *Leviathan* (1651), John Locke's *Two Treatises on Government* (1689), and Jean-Jacques Rousseau's *The Social Contract* (1762).

11 Douglass C. North (1990) *Institutions, Institutional Change and Economic Performance*, Cambridge University Press, p. 3.

12 This is the view of North (1990) which can also be traced back to political theorists of the seventeenth and eighteenth centuries. A classification of New Institutional Economics (NIE) even goes as far as claiming that institutions *are* property rights, since property rights can be viewed as kinds of contracts, conventions, and as governance structures.

Chapter 2   Policy and Politics of Land and Property

1 Daron Acemoglu, Simon Johnson, James Robinson (2004) *Institutions as the Fundamental Cause of Long-Run Growth*, NBER Working Paper No. 10481, National Bureau of Economic Research.

2 Healthy institutions can be viewed as a measure of the degree of informality. Specifically, the degree of informality equals the gap between written institutions and society's demands.

3 William Easterly and Ross Levine: *Tropics, Germs, and Crops – How Endowments Influence Economic Development*, NBER Working Paper 9106, National Bureau of Economic Research.

4 Acemoglu et al. (2004); loc. cit., p. 20.

5 Derived from mission statements of the International Monetary Fund (www.imf.org) and the World Bank (www.worldbank.org).

6 Toshihiko Kawagoe (1999) *Agricultural Land Reform in Postwar Japan*, Policy Research Working Paper No. 2111, World Bank Development Research Group, Policy Research Dissemination Center, Washington: World Bank.

7 This opinion is shared by many scholars, analysts and academics, and was confirmed to me in interviews with Arthur Domike (July of 2005). Arthur Domike is an economist and former land reform officer of the UN Food and Agriculture Organization.

8   Toshihiko Kawagoe (1999); loc. cit., p. 33.

9   Ronald P. Dore (1959) *Land Reform in Japan*, London: Oxford University Press, pp. 80–5, 106–12.

10 Wolf Isaac Ladejinsky (1977) *Agrarian Reform as Unfinished Business – The Selected Papers of Wolf Ladejinsky*, New York: Oxford University Press.

11 Ronald P. Dore (1960) *Shinchugun no Nochikaikaku Koso – Rekishi no Ichidanmen* (Land reform plan of SCAP – A historical sketch), Nogyo Sogo Kenkyu (*Quarterly Journal of Agricultural Economy*), Vol. 14(1), Tokyo: National Research Institute of Agricultural Economics, pp. 175–94.

12 Toshihiko Kawagoe (1999); loc. cit., p. 54.

13 Rosemary Thorp (1998) *Progress, Poverty and Exclusion – An Economic History of Latin America in the Twentieth Century*, Inter-American Development Bank, p. 140.

14 John F. Kennedy (1961) *Address at the White House Reception for Members of Congress and for the Diplomatic Corps of the Latin American Republics*, March 13th, 1961 in Theodore Sorensen (ed.) (1998) *Let the World Go Forth, The Speeches, Statements and Writings of John F. Kennedy*, New York: Delacorte Press, p. 352.

15 William Thiesenhusen (1989) *Agrarian Reform in Latin America*, Boston: Unwin Hyman, pp. 10 and 488. Thiesenhusen estimates that Peru appropriated and distributed 39 percent of its agricultural land, Panama 22 percent, Venezuela 19 percent the Dominican Republic 14 percent, Chile 10 percent, and Ecuador 9 percent.

16 Arthur Domike (2005) *The Revolution that Never Happened – Agrarian Reform and the Alliance for Progress*, unpublished paper presented at the Colloquium of the Esquel Group Foundation. June 23, 2005, Inter-American Development Bank.

17 Rosemary Thorp (1998); loc. cit., p. 140.

18 Ibid., p. 141.

19 Cadastre, from the Greek "*katastichon*," the use of which goes back to antiquity. Cadastres record information in an indexed manner and could be compared to a "telephone book" of property rights. In the case of real property, a cadastre takes the form of an official map that records information about the physical and geographic dimensions of a lot (rows and lines); it can also record information on ownership and use.

20 An overview of development paradigms following the Second World War can be found in Louka T. Katseli (2004) *Setting Priorities in Development Cooperation – A Short Overview of an*

Evolving Paradigm, Bruno Kreisky Forum for International Dialogue, Vienna.

21 Hyperinflation describes an inflationary cycle without a tendency towards equilibrium. Money loses its value at such a quick rate that it can no longer be a reliable medium of exchange – it practically becomes worthless. There is no formal definition as to when the devaluation of money must be called hyperinflation – typically inflation rates above 50 percent a month are called hyperinflation. Disregarding the exact definition of hyperinflation, the loss of monetary stability has serious consequences for an economy. Countries which have experienced hyperinflation include Germany in the 1920s, as well as many Latin American countries in the late 1980s and early 1990s (e.g. Argentina [3,080%], Bolivia [11,750%], Brazil [2,948%], and Peru [7,486%] number in brackets indicate the peak inflation rate in each country).

22 Barry Eichengreen and Ricardo Haussman (1999) *Exchange Rates and Financial Fragility*, NBER Working Paper No. 7418, National Bureau of Economic Research.

23 John Williamson of the Institute for International Economics is credited with coining this phrase. See his 1990 article on *What Washington Means by Policy Reform*, Institute for International Economics. The original list of ten policy recommendations also called for legal security of property rights. However, such institutional reforms were not tackled under actual Washington Consensus policies while the term became a synonym of neoliberal economic intervention.

24 Structural adjustment can be described as a set of policy measures designed to generate macroeconomic stability and economic growth.

25 *Brady bonds* are Dollar denominated bonds, named after US Treasury Secretary Nicholas Brady. They were created beginning 1989 under a US plan to transform non-performing commercial bank debt – reducing sovereign debt service of highly indebted countries such as Argentina, Mexico, and Venezuela into tradable securities.

26 A *currency board* is an automatic monetary rule, with all domestic money backed by foreign exchange reserves, and no independent monetary policy. Domestic currency is convertible at a fixed exchange rate with another currency (usually an "anchor" currency like the US Dollar or the Euro). A specific type of cur-

rency board is the gold standard, which sets the exchange rate of a currency relative to a specified weight of gold.

27 John Williamson has continuously pointed out how the initial list of ten policy recommendations was watered down and modified in actual policy implementation, which may explain some of the later difficulties experienced with the reforms. In fact, Williamson suggests dropping the term altogether because it has taken on such a different meaning. See John Williamson (2003) "From Reform Agenda to Damaged Brand Name", in *Finance and Development*, Vol. 40(3), Washington: IMF, pp. 10–13.

28 IMF World Economic Outlook Database, Washington: IMF. Argentina applied a currency board while Mexico and Brazil used a crawling peg regime.

29 Anoop Singh, Agnès Belaisch, Charles Collyns, Paula De Masi, Reva Krieger, Guy Meredith, Robert Rennhack (2005) *Stabilization and Reform in Latin America – A Macroeconomic Perspective on the Experience since the early 1990s*, Washington: IMF.

30 Anne-Marie Gulde (1999) "The Role of the Currency Board in Bulgaria's Stabilization", in *Finance and Development*, Vol. 36(3), Washington: IMF.

31 Moises Naim (1994) "Latin America – The Second Stage of Reforms", *Journal of Democracy*, pp. 33–48.

32 IMF (2003) *World Economic Outlook*, Washington: IMF. Also, Andreas Papandreou (1998) *Externality and Institutions*, Oxford University Press: Oxford, provides a penetrating account of mainstream economics' shortcomings deriving from its blindness to the centrality of institutions. With his work on *Institutional Economics – Its Place in Political Economy by* John R. Commons (1934) New York: Macmillan CO., pp. xiv, 921, became an early proponent of "institutional economics". For a recent survey of institutional economics with its many forms see Rutherford (2001) *Institutional Economics – Then and Now*, Malcolm Rutherford, *Journal of Economic Perspectives*, Vol. 15(3), Summer, 2001, pp. 173–94.

33 This change can be seen in a series of publications beginning in the late 1990s, including several World Development Reports (WDR) WDR 1997 *The State in a Changing World*, the 1998 viewpoint publication of Javed S. Burki and Guillermo E. Perry *Beyond the Washington Consensus – Institutions Matter*, The World Bank Latin American and Caribbean Studies; the 2002 WDR

Building Institutions for Markets, as well as the IMF's World Economic Outlooks (WEO) of 2003 and 2005.

34　John Harris, Janet Hunter, Colin M. Lewis (2000) *New Institutional Economics and Third World Development*, New York: Routledge Economics, p. 19.

35　Max Weber (1968) *Economy and Society*, ed. by Guenther Roth and Claus Wittich, New York: Bedminister Press.

36　De Soto (2000) gives out some examples of the extent of informal property in various countries: e.g. Philippines 57 percent urban and 67 percent rural; Egypt 92 percent urban and 83 percent rural.

Chapter 3　Tipping Points

1　Meets and bounds is a legal description of a parcel of land. A typical example would be: "From the point on the north bank of Rock Creek one kilometer above the junction of Rock Creek and Potomac River, north for 350 meters, then northwest to the large standing rock, west to the large oak tree, south to Rock Creek, then down the center of the creek to the starting point."

2　The concept of "social capital" was introduced by Jane Jacobs in the 1960s, but only received wide recognition when it was adopted by Pierre Bourdieu in 1983. In 2000, it became particularly well known through Robert D. Putnam's book *Bowling Alone – The Collapse and Revival of American Community*, New York: Simon & Schuster.

3　Francis Fukuyama (1995) *Trust – The Social Virtues and the Creation of Prosperity*, London: Penguin.

4　Game Theory became a prominent branch of applied mathematics in the 1940s, especially after the work of John von Neumann and Oskar Morgenstern on *The Theory of Games and Economic Behavior* which also introduced the theory to other disciplines. Game Theory studies strategic situations in which players have to choose between different actions in order to maximize their returns. It often demonstrates the inability of players to achieve optimal outcomes through lack of cooperation (e.g. "Prisoner's Dilemma"). Today, Game Theory is widely used in biology, computer sciences, political science, and especially economics (illustrated by the fact that the 2005 Nobel Prize for Economics was awarded to two game theorists, Thomas Schelling and Robert Aumann).

17 The term *terratenientes* was used for owners of very large estates while *gamonales* described people who managed operations for *terratenientes* and who occasionally owned small properties.
18 Norman Gall (1967) *Peru's Misfired Guerrilla Campaign*, The Reporter, January 26, 1967, p. 36.
19 Law Decree 17716, June 23, 1969.
20 William Thiesenhusen (1989) *Agrarian Reform in Latin America*, Boston: Unwin Hyman.
21 Communal land in Peru existed in two forms: *comunidades campesinas* and *comunidades indigenas*. Some of these communal lands were created by the Spanish before the founding of the Peruvian republic. Others – especially *comunidades campesinas* – were established after the 1969 Agrarian Reform.
22 Mateen Thobani (1995) *Peru – A User Based Approach to Water Management and Irrigation Development*, Report No. 13642-PE, Washington: World Bank, p. 4.
23 Cantuarias and Delgado (2004) loc. cit.
24 Thobani (1995) loc. cit., p. 4.
25 Thobani (1995) loc. cit., p. 3; Powelson and Stock (1990) loc. cit., p. 270; Thorp and Bertram (1978) loc. cit., p. 275.
26 CVR (2003) *Informe Final* (Final report), technical report, Comisión de la Verdad y Reconciliación (Truth and Reconciliation Commission), Lima: CVR.
27 That is, risk that economic or political instability in a country will interfere with the country's ability to meet its financial obligations (in this case, to international lenders).
28 World Bank (1998) PAD, loc. cit., and Cantuarias and Delgado (2004) loc. cit.
29 Instituto Libertad y Democracia (1993) *Peru – Pilot Project on the System for Titling and Registration of Informal Property*, Final Report, December 1993, Lima: ILD.
30 The success was especially apparent in comparison with efforts in other countries that had sought to establish property rights (such as in the case of the *Treuhand* in Eastern Germany). The number of formal property registrations in Peru outreached most of what was seen elsewhere and had followed recommendations coming from bad previous experiences. See Daniel Wachter and John English (1992) *The World Bank's Experience with Rural Land Titling*, The Environment Department, Policy and Research Divisional Working Paper No. 1992–35, Washington: World Bank.

Chapter 5   Results through Partnerships

1 World Bank (1998) PAD, loc. cit.
2 In 1992, the Peruvian government established a commission for privatizing state owned companies called COPRI (Comisión de Privatización) headed by Jaime Yoshiyama. The initiative was considered to be a very successful reform program. World Bank (1994) *Peru – A Private Sector Assessment*, Latin American and Caribbean Region, Report No. 12096-PE, Washington: World Bank.
3 World Bank (1998) PAD, loc. cit. See also Cantuarias and Delgado (2004) loc. cit.
4 Erica Field (2002) loc. cit.
5 Bank of America is second largest bank in terms of market capitalization.
6 Presentation by Brian Tracey, Bank of America Senior Vice President, at the "Spain – United States Forum on Public Private Partnerships in Financing Urban and Community Development," January 14 and 15, 2004 in Avila, Salamanca, and Madrid.
7 The National Council of *La Raza*, the largest national Hispanic civil rights and advocacy organization in the United States, works to improve opportunities for Hispanic Americans. Founded in 1968, it is a private, non-profit, non-partisan, tax-exempt organization headquartered in Washington, DC.
8 *Washington Post*, Dec. 15, 2005, p. B5.

Chapter 6   Solving the Puzzle

1 According to World Bank statistics (e.g. World Development Indicators, 2005), the percentage of people living on less than US$2 a day increased from 22.6 percent in 1996 to 36.2 percent in 1998.
2 Rent-seeking behavior must be distinguished from profit-seeking behavior in that it does not only include the quest for economic profit (which is justified through production costs and the price consumers are willing to pay), but some extra yield which rent-seekers can acquire based on a specific position of power. Rent-seeking is generally associated with monopolies that can charge a higher price due to a lack of competition in a specific industry. In this respect, rent-seeking is closely linked with the moral hazard phenomenon and asymmetry of information discussed above.

3 The economic crisis of 1998, which started as a financial tumult in the aftermath of the Asian crisis, led to a significant devaluation of the ruble and the default of public and private debt.

4 IMF Economic Outlook Database. 1998 percentage change of GDP was –5.3

5 The term was used in the World Bank's Country Assistance Evaluation of 2000, but indeed represented conventional wisdom at the time. World Bank (2000) Country Assistance Evaluation – Albania, loc. cit.

6 Christopher Jarvis (2000) "The Rise and Fall of Albania's Pyramid Schemes", in *Finance and Development*, Vol. 37(1), Washington: IMF.

7 Numbers from IMF: The Word Economic Outlook Database, Washington, DC: IMF.

8 By the present day, approximately 25 percent of the total population, or over 35 percent of the labor force, has emigrated. The country has approximately 900,000 emigrants, now residing mainly in Greece (600,000), Italy (200,000), and most of the remainder in other Western European countries, the US, and Canada. Albania's migration flow has, since the early 1990s, been five times higher than the average migration flow in developing countries.

9 Jarvis (2000) loc. cit.

Bibliography

A World Bank Policy Research Report (2003) Land Policies for Growth and Poverty Reduction, A publication of the World Bank and Oxford University Press.

Acemoglu, Daron and James A. Robinson (2006) *Economic Origins of Dictatorship and Democracy*, New York: Cambridge University Press.

Acemoglu, Daron, Simon Johnson and James Robinson (2004) 'Institutions as the Fundamental Cause of Long-Run Growth', NBER Working Paper No. 10481, National Bureau of Economic Research.

Akerloff, George (1970) 'The Market for Lemons – Quality Uncertainty and the Market Mechanism', in *Quarterly Journal of Economics*, Vol. 84, No. 3, 488–500.

Alesina, Alberto and Dani Rodrik (1994) 'Distributive Politics and Economic Growth', in *Quarterly Journal of Economics*, Vol. 109, S. 465–90.

Alston, Lee, Thrainn Eggertsson and Douglass C. North (1996) *Empirical Studies in Institutional Change*, New York: Cambridge University Press.

Andreas, A. Papandreou (1998) *Externality and Institutions*, Oxford: Oxford University Press.

Angel, S. (2001) 'Comments on Hernando De Soto's *The Mystery of Capital*', contribution to an electronic round-table arranged by the International Division of the American Planning Association.

Anne-Marie Gulde (1999) 'The Role of the Currency Board in Bulgaria's Stabilization', in *Finance and Development*, Vol. 36(3), Washington: IMF.

Anoop Singh, Agnès Belaisch, Charles Collyns, Paula De Masi, Reva Krieger, Guy Meredith, Robert Rennhack (2005), "Stabilization and Reform in Latin America: A Macroeconomic Perspective on the Experience Since the Early 1990's" IMF Survey Vol. 34, No. 3 paper No. 238, Washington: IMF.

Apoyo (2001) 'Encuesta de Linea Base – Proyecto Derechos de Propriedad Urbana', *Apoyo Consultoria*, Lima, Peru, January.

Atuahene, Bernadette (2004) 'Legal Title to Land as an Intervention Against Urban Poverty in Developing Nations', *The George Washington International Law Review*, Vol. 36, No. 5.

Bairoch, Paul (1993) *Economics and World History Myths and Paradoxes*, Chicago: University of Chicago Press.

Barbosa, Joao de Lucena and Tulio Barbosa (1992) 'Report on ILD Land Titling Project', internal working paper used for the preparation of the Peru Urban Property Rights project, Washington: The World Bank, April 1992.

Barnes, A. (2006) *Owning Russia: The Struggle over Factories, Farms and Power*, Ithaca, N.Y.: Cornell University Press.

Barraclough, Solon L. and Arthur L. Domike (November 1966) 'Agrarian Structure in Seven Latin American Countries' *Land Economics*, a quarterly journal devoted to the study of economic and social institutions, Vol. XLII, No. 4. The University of Wisconsin Press.

Barry Eichengreen and Ricardo Haussman (1999) *Exchange Rates and Financial Fragility*, NBER Working Paper No. 7418, National Bureau of Economic Research.

Bates, Robert H. (1995) 'Social Dilemmas and Rational Individuals – An Assessment of the New Institutionalism', in John Harris, Jante Hunter, Colin M. Lewis (eds) *The New Institutional Economics and Third World Development*, London/New York: Routledge, S. pp. 27–48.

Bentham, Jeremy (1802) 'Principles of the Civil Code', in *The Theory of Legislation*, ed. from Charles K. Ogden, London: Kegan Paul, 1931.

Boloña Behr, Carlos (1999) *La Privatización en el Perú – Costos y Beneficios*, Gestion June 14th, 1999.

Boloña Behr, Carlos (2000) *Experiencias Para una Economia al Servicio de la Gente*, Nuevas Technical Educativas S.A.C. NUTESA, Av. Republica de Panama, 2197 Of. 2B Lima-13-Peru.

Bourdieu, Pierre (1983) 'The forms of capital', in J.C. Richards (ed.) *Handbook of Theory and Research for the Sociology of Education*, New York: Greenwood Press.

Bourricaud, Francois (1970) *Power and Society in Contemporary Peru*, London: Faber and Faber.

Brian Tracey, Bank of America senior vice president, at the 'Spain – United States Forum on Public Private Partnerships in Financing Urban and Community Development', January 14 and 15, 2004 presentation in Avila, Salamanca, and Madrid.

Burki, Javed S. and Guillermo E. Perry (1998) *Beyond the Washington Consensus – Institutions Matter*, a publication of The World Bank Latin American and Caribbean Region.

Calem, Paul S. and Susan M. Wachter (1997) 'Community Reinvestment and Credit Risk: Evidence from an Affordable Home Loan Program' Wharton School Samuel Zell and Robert Lurie Real

Estate Center, University of Pennsylvania Zell/Lurie Center, Working Papers No. 306.

Carter, William H., Michael H. Schill and Susan M. Wachter (undated) 'Polarization and Public Housing in the United States', Wharton School Samuel Zell and Robert Lurie Real Estate Center, University of Pennsylvania Zell/Lurie Center, Working Papers No. 308.

Jarvis, Christopher (2000) 'The Rise and Fall of Albania's Pyramid Schemes', in *Finance and Development*, Vol. 37(1), Washington: IMF.

Coase, Ronald H. 1988, *The Firm, The Market, and the Law*, Chicago: University of Chicago Press, reprint ed. 1990.

Coase, Ronald H. (1937) 'The Nature of the Firm', *Economica*, 4, S. 386–405.

Coase, Ronald H. (1960) 'The Problem of Social Cost', in *Journal of Law and Economics*, 3, S. 1–44.

Collier, David (1976) *Squatters and Oligarchs – Authoritarian Rule and Policy Change in Peru*, Baltimore: Johns Hopkins University Press.

Commons, John R. (1931) 'Institutional Economics', in *American Economic Review*, Vol. 21, S. 648–57.

Commons, John R. (1934) *Institutional Economics – Its Place in Political Economy*, New York: Macmillan Co., pp. xiv, 921.

Conger, Lucy (1999) 'Entitled to Prosperity', in *Urban Age – The Global City Magazine*, Vol. 7(2), S. 7–11.

CVR (2003) *Informe Final* (Final report), technical report, Comisión de la Verdad y Reconciliación (Truth and Reconciliation Commission), Lima: CVR.

Davis, Kevin and Michael J. Trebilcock (1999) 'What Role do Legal Institutions Play in Development?', Working Paper prepared for the International Monetary Fund's Conference on Second Generation Reforms, 8–9 November, Washington, D.C.: International Monetary Fund.

De Soto, Hernando (1993) 'The Missing Ingredient', in *The Economist*, Vol. 328, Nr. 7828, Special Supplement for the Economist's 150 years, 11 September 1993, S. 10–14.

De Soto, Hernando (2000a) *The Mystery of Capital: Why Capitalism Triumphs in the West and Fails Everywhere Else*, New York: Basic Books.

De Soto, Hernando (2000b) *The Other Path*, New York: Perseus Books Group; Reprint edition (September 3, 2002).

Deininger, Klaus and Gershon Feder (1999) 'Land Policy in Developing Countries', *Rural Development* No. 20876, Washington: The World Bank.

Deininger, Klaus and Hans Binswanger (1999) 'The Evolution of the World Bank's Land Policy – Principles, Experience, and Future Challenges', in *The World Bank Research Observer*, Vol. 14(2), S. 247–76.

Demsetz, Harold (1967) 'Toward A Theory of Property Rights', in *American Economic Review*, Vol. 57, Mai 1967, American Economic Association, S. 347–59.

Diamond, Jared (1997) *Guns, Germs, and Steel: The Fates of Human Societies*. New York: W.W. Norton & Company.

Dieckmann, Oliver (1996) 'Cultural Determinants of Economic Growth – Theory and Evidence', in *Journal of Cultural Economics*, Vol. 20(4), New York: Kluwer Academic Publishers, S. 285–308.

Domike, Arthur (2005) 'The Revolution that Never Happened – Agrarian Reform and the Alliance for Progress', unpublished paper presented at the Colloquium of the Esquel Group Foundation. June 23, 2005, Inter-American Development Bank.

Dore, Ronald P. (1959) *Land Reform in Japan*, London: Oxford University Press.

Dore, Ronald P. (1960) 'Shinchugun no Nochikaikaku Koso – Rekishi no Ichidanmen' (Land reform plan of SCAP – A historical sketch), *Nogyo Sogo Kenkyu* (*Quarterly Journal of Agricultural Economy*), Vol. 14(1), Tokyo: National Research Institute of Agricultural Economics.

Easterly, William (2001) *The Elusive Quest for Growth – Economists' Adventures and Misadventures in the Tropics*, Boston: MIT Press.

Easterly, William and Ross Levine (2002) 'Tropics, Germs, and Crops – How Endowments Influence Economic Development', NBER Working Paper 9106; National Bureau of Economic Research.

Easterly, William (2006) *The White Man's Burden: Why the West's Efforts to Aid the Rest Have Done So Much Ill and So Little Good*, New York: Penguin Press.

Easterly, William, Jozef Ritzen and Michael Woolcock (2006) 'Social Cohesion, Institutions, and Growth' *Economics and Politics*, 18(2), July: 103–20.

Economist (12/21/96) 'Full Democracy – It means government by the people, and we are the people'.

Economist (January/29/2004) 'Peru's Gastronomic Revolution'.

Economist (August/24/2006) 'Of property and poverty.

Ekelund, Robert B. Jr. and Robert Tollison (1981) *Mercantilism as a Rent-Seeking Society*, College State: Texas A&M University Press.

Ellickson, Robert C. (1991) *Order Without Law – How Neighbors Settle Disputes*, Cambridge: Harvard University Press.

Engels, Friedrich (1986) *The Origin of the Family, Private Property and the State*, Penguin Classics, with introduction by Michele Barette; first published in 1884.

English, John and Daniel Wachter (1992) 'The World Bank's Experience with Rural Land Titling', The Environment Department, Working Paper No. 1992–35 of the Policy Research Division, Washington: The World Bank.

English, Philip C. and William T. Moore (2002) 'Property Rights Ambiguity and the Effect of Foreign Direct Investment Decisions on Firm Value', in Gerald O'Driscoll, Kim R. Holmes, Mary Anastasia O'Grady (eds) *2002 Index of Economic Freedom*, The Heritage Foundation, Washington: The Wall Street Journal.

Expreso (2000) 'Títulos de Cofopri: legalment impecables, pero tienen poco valor para los bancos', in *Expreso*, 23 July, pp. 4–5.

Fafchamps, Marcel (1996) 'The Enforcement of Commercial Contracts in Ghana', *World Development*.

Fafchamps, Marcel and Bart Minten (1999) 'Property Rights in a Flea Market Economy', Oxford, UK: CSAE WPS/99–25.

Feder, Gershon, Tongroj Onchan, Yongyuth Chalamwong and Chira Hongladarom (1988) *Land Policy and Farm Productivity in Thailand*, Baltimore: The Johns Hopkins University Press.

Fernando, Cantuarias and Miguel Delgado (2004) 'Peru's Urban Land Titling Program', Scaling Up Poverty Reduction – A Global Learning Process and Conference, Shanghai, May 25–27, 2004.

Field, Erica (2002) 'Entitled to Work – Urban Property Rights and Labor Supply in Peru', Working Paper, Princeton University, Industrial Relations Section, electronic version under www.princeton.edu/~emfield.

Field, Erica (2002) *Entitled to Work – Urban Property Rights and Labor Supply in Peru*, Princeton Law & Public Affairs Working Paper No. 02–1.

Fukuyama, Francis (1995) *Trust – The Social Virtues and the Creation of Prosperity*, London: Penguin.

Fukuyama, Francis (2002) 'Culture and Economic Development,' from the Encyclopedia of the Social and Behavioral Sciences, Elsevier.

Fukuyama, Francis (2004) *State Building: Governance and World Order in the 21st Century*, Ithaca, NY: Cornell University Press.

Furubotn, Erik G. and Rudolf Richter (1997) *Institutions and Economic Theory – The Contribution of the New Institutional Economics*, Ann Arbor: University of Michigan Press.

Gall, Norman (1967) 'Peru's Misfired Guerrilla Campaign', *The Reporter*, January 26, 1967.

Gladwell, Malcolm (2000) *The Tipping Point – How Little Things Can Make a Big Difference*, New York: Back Bay Books.

Gopal, G. (1999) *Gender-Related Legal Reform and Access to Economic Resources in Eastern Africa*, Washington D.C.: The World Bank Publications.

Grodzins, Morton (1957) 'Metropolitan Segregation', *Scientific American*, 197, October.

Grossman, Herschel I. (2001) 'The Creation of Effective Property Rights', *American Economic Review*, Vol. 91(2), S. 347–52.

Hargadon, Andrew (2003) *How Breakthroughs Happen*, Boston: Harvard Business School Press.

Harpum, C., M. Grant and S. Bridge (2000) *The Law of Real Property*, *Sixth Edition*, London: Sweet & Maxwell.

Harris, John, Janet Hunter, Colin M. Lewis (1995) 'Introduction – Development and Significance of NIE': The New Institutional Economics and Third World Development, London/New York: Routledge, S. 1–16.

Harris, John, Janet Hunter, Colin M. Lewis (2000) *New Institutional Economics and Third World Development*, New York: Routledge Economics.

Hayek, Friedrich A. (1960) *The Constitution of Liberty*, Chicago: The University of Chicago Press.

Heckscher, Eli F. (1955) *Mercantilism*, London: George Allen and Unwin, 2 vol. revised second edition, ed. by Ernst F. Söderlund. (Originally published as *Merkantilisment: Ett led i den ekonomiska politikens historia*. Stockholm: P.A. Norstedt and Söner, 1931)

Heiner, Ronald (1983) 'The Origins of Predictable Behavior', *American Economic Review*, 75: 560–95.

Herbert, Simon (1991) 'Organizations and Markets', *Journal of Economic Perspectives*, 5(2).

Herbst, Kris (2002) 'Enabling the Poor to Build Housing: Cemex Combines Profit and Social Development', *Changemakers Journal*, September/October.

Hobbes, Thomas (1651) *Leviathan*, Stuttgart: Reclam, 1980.

Hodess R., T. Inowlocki and T. Wolfe (2003) *Global Corruption Report 2003: Access to Information*, London: Profile Books Ltd/Transparency International.

Hogarth, Robin M., and Melvin W. Reder (eds) (1986) *Rational Choice*, Chicago and London: The University of Chicago Press.

Home, R. and Lim, H. (eds) (2004) *Demystifying the Mystery of Capital: Land Tenure and Poverty in Africa and the Caribbean*, London: Cavendish Publishing.

Hoskins, Lee and Ana I. Eiras (2002) 'Property Rights – The Key to Economic Growth', in Gerald O'Driscoll, Kim R. Holmes, Mary Anastasia O'Grady (eds) 2002 Index of Economic Freedom, The Heritage Foundation, Washington: The Wall Street Journal, S. 37–48.

Hume, David (1739) 'A Treatise of Human Nature', in Thomas Hill Green and Thomas Hodge Grose (eds) *Hume – Philosophical Works*, Vol. 2, Aalen: Scientia Verlag, 1992, S. 73–374.

Hutchcroft, Paul D. (1998) *Booty Capitalism – The Politics of Banking in the Philippines*, Ithaca, NY: Cornell University Press.

Instituto Libertad y Democracia (1993) 'Peru – Pilot Project on the System for Titling and Registration of Informal Property', Final Report, December 1993, Lima: ILD.

International Monetary Fund (2003) *World Economic Outlook*, Washington: IMF.

International Monetary Fund (2005) *World Economic Outlook*, Washington: IMF.

International Monetary Fund (2006) *World Economic Outlook Database*, Washington: IMF.

Jacobs, Jane (1961) *The Death and Life of Great American Cities*, New York: Random House.

Johnson, Simon, John McMillan and Christopher Woodruff (1999) 'Property Rights, Finance and Entrepreneurship', Working Paper No. 43 European Bank for Reconstruction and Development, London: EBRD.

Kagawa, Ayako (2001) 'Policy Effects and Tenure Security Perceptions of Peruvian Urban Land Tenure Regularisation Policy in the 1990s', working paper for the conference 'Cooping With Informality and Illegality in Human Settlements in Developing Cities,' European Science Foundation (ESF), 23–26 May 2001, Brussels, Belgium.

Kälin, C.H. (2005) *International Real Estate Handbook: Acquisition, Ownership and Sale of Real Estate Residence, Tax and Inheritance Law*, Chichester: John Wiley & Sons Ltd.

Katseli, Louka T. (2004) 'Setting Priorities in Development Co-operation – A Short Overview of an Evolving Paradigm', Bruno Kreisky Forum for International Dialogue, Vienna.

Kawagoe, Toshihiko (1999) 'Agricultural Land Reform in Postwar Japan: Experiences and Issues', Policy Research Working Paper No. 2111, World Bank Development Research Group, Policy Research Dissemination Center, Washington: The World Bank.

Keefer, Philip and Stephen Knack (2000) 'Polarization, Politics and Property Rights – Links Between Inequality and Growth', Working Paper No. 2418, Washington: The World Bank.

Kennedy, John F. (1961) 'Address at the White House Reception for Members of Congress and for the Diplomatic Corps of the Latin American Republics', March 13th, 1961 from Theodore Sorensen (ed.) (1998) *Let the World Go Forth, The Speeches, Statements and Writings of John F. Kennedy*, New York: Delacorte Press.

Kim, Chan W. and Renee Mauborgne (1999) 'Creating New Market Space', *Harvard Business Review* 75, January–February, 102–12.

Kim, Chan W. and Renee Mauborgne (2005) *Blue Ocean Strategy: How to Create Uncontested Market Space and Make the Competition Irrelevant*, Boston, Massachusetts: Harvard Business School Publishing Corporation.

Klitgaard, Robert, Parris Maclean-Abaroa and Ronald H. Linsey (2000) *Corrupt Cities: A Practical Guide to Care and Prevention*, Institute of Contemporary Studies Press, Oakland, California USA: World Bank Institute, Washington D.C.

Klitggard, Robert (1994) Ajustandonos a la Realidad, Sudamericana.

Knack, Stephen and Philip Keefer (1997) 'Does Social Capital Have an Economic Payoff? A Cross-Country Investigation', in *The Quarterly Journal of Economics*, Vol. 112(4), S. 1251–88.

Lacy, John Q. (1984) 'Historical Overview of the Mining Law: The Miner's law Becomes Law', in *The Mining Law of 1872*, Washington, D.C.: National Legal Center for the Public Interest.

Lall, Subir, Nikola Spatafora and Martin Sommer (2005) 'Building Institutions', Chapter 3, *World Economic Outlook*, Washington D.C.: International Monetary Fund.

Landes, Daniel S. (1990) 'Why Are We So Rich and They So Poor?', in *American Economic Review*, Vol. 80(2), S. 1–13.

Lane, Jan Erik and Svant Ersson (2000) *The New Institutional Politics – Performance and Outcomes*, London/New York: Routledge.

Lanjouw, Jean O. and Philip I. Levy (2002) 'Untitled – A Study of Formal and Informal Property Rights in Urban Ecuador', in *Economic Journal*, Vol. 112(482), S. 986–1019.

Locke, John (1764) *Two Treatises of Government*, ed. Thomas Hollis (London: A. Millar et al.).

Macpherson, Crawford Brough (ed.) (1978) 'The Meaning of Property', in *Property – Mainstream and Critical Position*, Oxford: Blackwell, S. 1–13.

Macpherson, Crawford Brough (ed.) (1978) *Property – Mainstream and Critical Position*, Oxford: Blackwell, S. 41–58.

Mallaby, Sebastian (2004) *The World Banker*, NY: The Penguin Press.

Mandelbaum, M. (2002) *The Ideas that Conquered the World: Peace, Democracy, Free Markets in the Twenty First Century*, New York: Public Affairs.

March, James G. and Johan P. Olson (1989) *Rediscovering Institutions – The Organizational Basis of Politics*, New York: Free Press.

McLaughlin, John and David Palmer (1996) 'Land Registration and Development', in *ITC Journal*, No. 96–1, S. 10–18.

McLaughlin, J.D. and S.E. Nichols (1989) 'Resource Management: The Land Administration and cadastral Systems Component,' *Surveying and Mapping*, Vol. 49 No. 2.

McLaughlin, John (1997) 'Integrated Land Administration – Institutional and Technical Challenges', http://www.gisqatar.org.qa/conf97/links/f2.html

Mill, John Stuart (1871) 'Principles of Political Economy with Some of Their Applications to Social Philosophy', 2. Buch, 7. Ausg., in: ders.: Collected Works of John Stuart Mill, Band 2, eds. von John M. Robson, London: Routledge and Kegan Paul, 1965.

Mission Statements of the International Monetary Fund and the World Bank, http://worldbank.org and http://www.imf.org.

Moises, Naim (1994) 'Latin America – The Second Stage of Reforms', *Journal of Democracy*.

Montúfar, G. (2002) 'Los Sistemas de Administración de Tierras en el Peru', Final report prepared for the World Bank.

Moore, James F. (1996) *The Death of Competition: Leadership and Strategy in the Age of Business Ecosystems*, New York: Harper Business.

Morris Guerinoni, Felipe (2004) *Develando el misterio: La formalizacion de la propiedad en el Peru*, Peru: Comission para la formalizacion de la Propiedad Informal.

Mueller, Dennis C. (1993) *Public Choice II – A revised Edition of Public Choice*, Press Syndicate of University of Cambridge.

Mueller, Dennis C. (1997) *Public Choice II – A Revised Edition of Public Choice*, Cambridge: Cambridge University Press.

North, Douglass C. (1981) *Structure and Change in Economic History*, New York: Norton.

North, Douglass C. (1987) 'Institutions, Transaction Costs and Economic Growth', in *Economic Inquiry*, Vol. 25(3), Oxford: Oxford University Press, S. 419–28.

North, Douglass C. (1990) *Institutions, Institutional Change and Economic Performance*, New York: Cambridge University Press.

North, Douglass C. (1995) 'The New Institutional Economics and Third World Development', in John Harris, Jante Hunter, Colin

M. Lewis (eds) *The New Institutional Economics and Third World Development*, London/New York: Routledge, S. 17–26.

North, Douglass C. (2005) *Understanding the Process of Economic Change*, Princeton, N.J.: Princeton University Press.

North, Douglass C. and Robert P. Thomas (1973) *The Rise of the Western World: A New Economic History*, Cambridge: Cambridge University Press.

North, Douglass C. (1990a–2003) *Institutions, Institutional Change, and Economic Performance*, New York: Cambridge University Press.

North, Douglass C. (1990b) 'A Transactions Cost Theory of Politics', *Journal of Theoretical Politics*, October 2, 4: 355–67.

North, Douglass C. (1994) 'Economic Performance Through Time', *American Economic Review*, Vol. 84, No. 3, June: 359–67.

Noyes, Reynold C. (1936) *The Institution of Property*, New York: Longman's Green.

Olson, Mancur (2000) *Power and Prosperity Outgrowing Communist and Capitalist Dictatorships*, New York: Basic Books.

Original version [DE SOTO, Hernando (1989) The Other Path – The Invisible Revolution in the Third World, New York: Harper & Row.]

Ostrom, Elinor (1990) *Governing the Commons: The Evolution of Institutions for Collective Action*, Cambridge: Cambridge University Press.

Panaritis, Elena (2001) 'Do Property Rights Matter? A case study from Peru,' in the *International Urban Research Monitor*, April 2001, Washington, D.C.: The Widow Wilson International Centre for Scholars.

Panaritis, Elena (2005) *Is Informality an Enigma? Informal Urban Property in Peru*, INSEAD Euro-Asia Centre, Research Series No. 79, July 2005, Paris: INSEAD.

Pipes, Richard (1999) *Property and Freedom*, New York: Alfred A. Knopf.

Pipes, Richard (2000) *Property and Freedom*, New York: Vintage.

Porter, Michael E. (1980) *Competitive Strategy*, New York: Free Press.

Porter, Michael E. (1985) *Competitive Advantage*, New York: Free Press.

Porter, Michael E. (1996) 'What is Strategy?', *Harvard Business Review* 74, November, December.

Posner, Richard (2002) *Economic Analysis of Law* (Aspen, 6th edition).

Powelson, John P. and Richard Stock (1987) *The Peasant Betrayed – Agriculture and Land Reform in the Third World*, Boston: Oelgeschlager, Gunn & Hain (chapter on Peru).

Powelson, John P. and Richard Stock (1990) *The Peasant Betrayed –
Agriculture and Land Reform in the Third World*, Washington: CATO
Institute.

Prahalad, C.K. (2006) *The Fortune at the Bottom of the Pyramid:
Eradicating Poverty Through Profits: Enabling Dignity and Choice
Through Markets*, Upper Saddle River, N.J.: Wharton School
Publishing.

Putnam, Robert D., Robert Leonardi and Raffaella Y. Nanetti (1994)
Making Democracy Work: Civic Traditions in Modern Italy, Princeton,
N.J.: Princeton University Press.

Putnam, Robert D. (1993) 'The Prosperous Community – Social
Capital and Public Life', in *American Prospect*, Vol. 13, S. 35–42.

Putnam, Robert D. (2000) *Bowling Alone – The Collapse and Revival of
American Community*, New York: Simon & Schuster.

Raiser, Martin (1997) 'Informal Institutions, Social Capital and
Economic Transition – Reflections on a Neglected Dimension',
Working Paper No. 25, The European Bank for Reconstruction
and Development, London: EBRD.

Razzaz, Omar M. (1993) 'Examining Property Rights and Investment
in Informal Settlements – The Case of Jordan', in *Land Economics*,
Vol. 69(4), S. 341–55.

Ritzen, Jozef, William Easterly and Michael Woolcock (2000) 'On
"Good" Politicians and "Bad" Policies – Social Cohesion,
Institutions and Growth', World Bank Working paper No. 2448,
Washington: The World Bank.

Roberts, Kenneth M. (1996) 'Neoliberalism and the Transformation
of Populism in Latin America: The Peruvian Case', in *World
Politics*, 48(1) 82–116.

Robinson, James A. and Daron Acemoglu (2000) 'The Colonial
Origins of Comparative Development: An Empirical Investigation', Working paper 7771, Washington, D.C.: NBER.

Rodrik, Dani (1999) 'Institutions for High-Quality Growth – What
They Are and How to Acquire Them', Arbeitspapier No. 7540, The
National Bureau of Economic Research, Cambridge: NBER.

Rousseau, Jean-Jacques (1755) 'Discours sur l'origine et le fonde-
ments de l'inégalité parmi les hommes', in Roger D. Masters (ed.)
The First and Second Discourses of Rousseau, New York: St Martin's
Press, 1964.

Rousseau, Jean-Jacques (1762) *Du Contrat Social – ou principes du droit
politique*, Amsterdam: Marc Michel Rey.

Rutherford, Malcolm (2001) *Journal of Economic Perspectives*, Vol.
15(3), Summer.

Schelling, Thomas (1984) *Choice and Consequence*, Harvard: Harvard University Press.

Schelling, Thomas C. (1971) 'Dynamic Models of Segregation', *Journal of Mathematical Sociology*, Vol. 1. (Abbreviated version appeared as 'Models of Segregation', in *The American Economic Review*, Vol. LIX, No. 2, May 1969.)

Schwab, Klaus and Claude Smadja (1999) 'Globalization Needs a Human Face', *International Herald Tribune*, January 28.

Sen, Amartya (1999) *Development as Freedom*, Oxford: Oxford University Press.

Simon, Herbert A. (1955) 'A Behavioral Model of Rational Choice', in *The Quarterly Journal of Economics*, No. 69, S. 99–118.

Simon, Herbert A. (1986) 'Rationality in Psychology and Economics', in Robin M. Hogarth and Melvin W. Reder (eds) *The Behavioral Foundations of Economic Theory, Journal of Business*, Vol. 59, S. 209–24.

Simon, Herbert (1986) 'Rationality in Psychology and Economics,' in Robin M. Hogarth and Melvin W. Reber (eds), *Rational Choice: The Contrast between Economics and Psychology*, Chicago: University of Chicago Press.

Solow, Robert M. (2000) 'Notes on Social Capital and Economic Performance', in Ismail Serageldin and Partha Dasgupta (eds), *Social Capital: A Multifaceted Perspective*, Washington, D.C.: The World Bank.

Soros, George (1998) *The Crisis of Global Capitalism; Open Society Endangered*, New York: Public Affairs.

Stern, Steve J. (ed.) (1998) *Shining and Other Paths: War and Society in Peru 1980–1995*, Durham and London: Duke University Press.

Stiglitz, Joseph E. (1998) 'Towards a New Paradigm for Development: Strategies, Policies, and Processes' (Geneva: 1998 Prebisch Lecture, UNCTAD).

Stiglitz, Joseph E. (1999) 'Knowledge as a Public Good', in Inge Kaul, Isabelle Grunberg and Marc A. Stern (eds) *Global Public Goods – International Cooperation in the 21st Century*, New York: Oxford University Press, S. 308–25.

Stiglitz, Joseph E. (2006) *Making Globalization Work*, New York: W.W. Norton.

The Economist (January/29/2004) 'Peru's Gastronomic Revolution', January 29th, 2004.

The Economist (August/24/2006) 'Of property and poverty' August 24, 2006.

The World Bank (2000) Anticorruption in Transition: a Contribution to the Policy Debate – a World Free of Poverty, Washington DC, The World Bank.

The World Bank (2003) The World Bank and Anticorruption in Europe and Central Asia: Enhancing Transparency, Voice and Accountability Washington DC, The World Bank.

The World Bank, Operational Core Services (OCS) Poverty Reduction and Economic Management (PREM) Network (June 2000) Helping Countries Combat Corruption – Progress and the World Bank since 1997.

Thiesenhusen, William (ed.) (1989) *Searching for Agrarian Reform in Latin America*, Boston: Unwin.

Thiesenhusen, William C. (1995) *Early Revolutionary Reforms: Bolivia, Broken Promises – Agrarian Reform and the Latin American Campesino*, Boulder: Colorado Westview Press.

Thobani, Mateen (1995) 'Peru – A User Based Approach to Water Management and Irrigation Development', Report No. 13642-PE. Washington: The World Bank.

Thorp, Rosemary (1998) 'Progress, Poverty and Exclusion – An Economic History of Latin America in the Twentieth Century', Inter-American Development Bank.

Thorp, Rosemary and Geoffrey Bertram (1978) *Peru 1890–1977 – Growth and Policy in an Open Economy*, London: Macmillan.

Tinker, I. and G. Summerfield (eds) (1999) *Women's Rights to House and Land: China, Laos, Vietnam*, Boulder: Lynne Rienner Publishers Inc.

Toye, John (1995) 'The New Institutional Economics and it's Implications for Development', in John Harris, Jante Hunter, Colin M. Lewis (eds) *The New Institutional Economics and Third World Development*, London/New York: Routledge, S. 49–70.

Turkstra, Jan, Ayako Kagawa, Nelly Amemiya (2000) 'Property Formalization and Guided Land Development in Peru', in *Storia Urbana*, Vol. 88/89, Mailand: Franco Agneli.

von Neumann, John and Oskar Morgenstern (1944) *The Theory of Games and Economic Behavior*, Princeton: Princeton University Press.

Wachter, Daniel and John English (1992) 'The World Bank's Experience with Rural Land Titling', The Environment Department, Policy and Research Divisional Working Paper No. 1992–35, Washington: The World Bank.

Wallis, Joe and Brian Dollery (1990) *Market Failure, Government Failure, Leadership and Public Policy*, New York: St. Martin's Press.

Wallis, John J. and Douglass C. North (1990) 'Institutional Change and Technical Change in American Economic Growth: A Transactions Costs Approach', *Journal of Institutional and Theoretical Economics*.

Washington Post, Dec. 15, 2005, p. B5.

Weber, Max (1904) 'Die protestantische Ethik und der Geist des Kapitalismus', found in Tübingen: J.C.B. Mohr (Paul Siebeck), University of Tübingen, 1988 (Erstveröff, 1920), S. 17–206.

Weber, Max (1968) *Economy and Society*, ed. by Guenther Roth and Claus Wittich, New York: Bedminister Press.

Williamson, O.E. (2000) 'The New Institutional Economics: Taking Stock, Looking Ahead', *Journal of Economic Literature*, Volume 38 pp. 595–613.

Williamson, Ian P. (2001) 'Land Administration "Best Practice" – Providing the Infrastructure for Land and Policy Implementation', in *Journal of Land Use Policy*, Vol. 18(4), S. 297–307.

Williamson, John (1990) 'What Washington Means by Policy Reform', in *Latin American Adjustment – How Much Has Happened?*, Washington: Institute for International Economics.

Williamson, John (2000) 'What Should the World Bank Think about the Washington Consensus?', *The World Bank Research Observer*, Vol. 15(2), August 2000, Washington: The World Bank, S. 251–64.

Williamson, John (1990) *What Washington Means by Policy Reform*, Institute for International Economics.

Williamson, John (2003) 'From Reform Agenda to Damaged Brand Name', in *Finance and Development*, Vol. 40(3), Washington: IMF.

Wolf, Isaac Ladejinsky (1977) *Agrarian Reform as Unfinished Business – The Selected Papers of Wolf Ladejinsky*, New York: Oxford University Press.

Woolcock, Michael (2004) 'Why and How Planners Should Take Social Capital Seriously', *Journal of the American Planning Association*, 70(2) May: 183–9.

Woolcock, Michael and Narayan Deepa (2006) 'Social Capital: Implications for Development Theory, Research, and Policy', *The Search for Empowerment: Social Capital as Idea and Practice at the World Bank*. Ed. Anthony Bebbington, Michael Woolcock, Scott Guggenheim and Elizabeth Olson. Kumarian Press, pp. 31–62.

World Bank (1989) *World Development Report*, Washington: The World Bank.

World Bank (1997) 'The State in a Changing World', *World Development Report*, Washington: The World Bank.

World Bank (1998) 'Final Report – Pre-Approval Quality at Entry Assessment Peru Urban Property Rights', Office Memorandum vol. 15. Jun 1998, Manuel Penalver-Quesada, Jaime Biderman, Gershon Feder, Geroge Wachtenheim, Washington: The World Bank.

World Bank (2000) 'Entering the 21st Century, World Development Report 1999/2000', Washington: The World Bank.

World Bank (2000a) *World Development Indicators 2000*, Washington: World Bank.

World Bank (2001) *Attacking Poverty, World Development Report 2000/01*, Washington: The World Bank.

World Bank (2002) *Building Institutions for Markets, World Development Report 2002*, Washington: The World Bank.

World Bank (1994) *Peru – A Private Sector Assessment*, Latin American and Caribbean Region, Report No. 12096-PE, Washington: World Bank.

World Bank (1998) Project Appraisal Document (PAD) on a Proposed Loan in the Amount of US$38 Million Equivalent to the Republic of Peru for an Urban Property Rights Project, Report No. 18245-PE, July 15, 1998, Washington: World Bank.

World Bank (1998) Quality at Entry Report, Quality Assurance Group (QAG), Washington: World Bank.

World Bank (1999) 'Peru, Urban Property Rights Program' Annual Meetings brochure.

World Bank (2000) Country Assistance Evaluation – Albania.

World Bank (2004) *World Development Report: Making Services Work for Poor People*, Washington, D.C.: Oxford University Press.

World Bank, IFC (2005) *Doing Business 2005: Removing Obstacles to Growth*, Oxford University Press. New York

World Bank, IFC (2006a) *Doing Business 2006: Creating Jobs*, Oxford University Press. New York

World Bank, IFC (2006b) *Doing Business 2007: How to Reform*, Oxford University Press. New York

World Bank (1997) *World Development Report: The State in a Changing World*, Oxford University Press and the World Bank. New York

World Bank/IBRD (2006) *Where is the Wealth of Nations? Measuring Capital for the 21st Century*, Washington D.C.: World Bank Publications.

World Development Indicators, 2005. Washington D.C.

World Development Report (2002) *Building Institutions for Markets*, Oxford University Press and the World Bank. New York

Young, Peyton H. (1998, 2001) *Individual Strategy and Social Structure: An Evolutionary Theory of Institutions*, Princeton New Jersey: Princeton University Press.

Young, Peyton H. (2004) *Dark Ages Ahead*, Toronto: Random House Canada.

Index

political leadership 121–2, 129–30
"politically sensitive" topics 26
private lenders 6, 103–4, 114, 115, 117
private sector 117, 141–2
privatization, Peru 70–1, 72
property construction materials 3
property improvement incentives 60
property law 35–6
property market 74–5, 82
property registry *see* registries
property rights 16–17, 41, 43
  institutions, organizations and 9–11
property rights reform 118–21
  consolidation of 134
  elements 131–2
  ingredients of secure system 53–6
  Peru, significance of 69–70
  principles 128–9, 133–4
  socioeconomic benefits 58–65, 106–13
  trust and reliability 48–53
  USA 118–21
  see also institutional reforms; registries
property transactions 47–8
  costs 5–6, 16, 59–60, 75, 122, 134
property values 62, 102, 109–11
public registration *see* registries
public services and utilities 64–5
Putnam, R. 49
pyramid schemes, Albania 138–41

quality controls 78, 106

real estate, definition 10
Reality Check Analysis 38–43, 58, 65, 72, 74–5, 102, 125–6, 130

records *see* registries; titles/certificates
registries
  importance of reliable 56–8
  pilot scheme 94–9
  Reality Check Analysis 72
  reformed 60, 62, 93–100 *passim*, 134
  see also titles/certificates
Registro de la Propiedad Inmueble 79
Registro Predial 60, 62, 93–4, 99, 104
reputation 49–50
resistance to change 36–7, 97–9, 132
resource management planning 65
revenue collection 65
Revolutionary Movement of Tupac Amaru (MRTA) 87–8, 97–8
risk and unreal estate 115
Rousseau, J.-J. 17, 18
rule of law 22, 32–3, 112
Russia
  post-communist 135–7
  see also Soviet Union

"second-generation reforms" 31–3
security, perceived 107–8
segmentation 25–31, 128
self-correcting system 134
self-reliance 27, 68
shared legitimacy 112
shared property ownership 63–4
Shining Path 87–8, 97–8
Smith, A. 8
social capital 48, 49, 51, 52, 75, 112
social contract 9, 17, 19, 20, 26, 63
social stability 64
socioeconomic benefits of reform 58–65, 106–13